D1594540

Thomas Merton and the Celts

Thomas Merton and the Celts

A New World Opening Up

Monica Weis SSJ

FOREWORD BY
Bonnie B. Thurston

☙PICKWICK *Publications* · Eugene, Oregon

THOMAS MERTON AND THE CELTS
A New World Opening Up

Pickwick Publications
An Imprint of Wipf and Stock Publishers
199 W. 8th Ave., Suite 3
Eugene, OR 97401

www.wipfandstock.com

PAPERBACK ISBN: 978–1-4982–7844–7
HARDCOVER ISBN: 978–1-4982–7846–1
EBOOK ISBN: 978-1-4982-8932-0

Cataloguing-in-Publication data:

Names: Weis, Monica, 1942–.

Title: Thomas merton and the Celts : a new world opening up / Monica Weis; foreword by Bonnie B. Thurston.

Description: Eugene, OR: Pickwick Publications, 2016 | Includes bibliographical references and index.

Identifiers: ISBN 978–1-4982–7844–7 (paperback) | ISBN 978–1-4982–7846–1 (hardcover) | ISBN 978-1-4982-8932-0 (ebook)

Subjects: LSCH: Merton, Thomas, 1915–1968 | Celtic Church | Christianity—Great Britain

Classification: BX4705.M542 W45 2016 (print) | BX4705.M542 (ebook)

Manufactured in the U.S.A.   09/16/16

Copyright notices

For Christine, Bonnie, and Patrick

who continue to inspire and guide me;

in fond memory of Donald Allchin,

who sowed Celtic seeds in my heart;

and with special gratitude to Esther deWaal

for her comprehensive contribution to the world of Celtic Studies.

The woodland birds might sing to him around his cell,
but through it all, rarely expressed, always implicit,
is the understanding that the bird and hermit
are joining together in an act of worship.

—KENNETH H. JACKSON

Contents

Foreword

Thomas Merton's interest in the Celtic is another example of his being "ahead of the curve" of popular interest in and attention to ideas and movements. In this, as in ecumenism, inter-religious dialogue, and some aspects of social justice, for example, Merton was a pioneer, not in the sense of a "trend setter," but as one who gave substance and depth to what later became a trend. And so it was with Merton and the Celtic tradition. He explored the Welsh roots of his family, read widely in serious, scholarly material (especially on Celtic monasticism), shared the fruit of that study with his novices, and engaged in epistolary friendships with several scholars of the Celtic world and its more contemporary manifestations. Monica Weis' engaging book breaks new ground in Merton studies as the first full-length examination of Merton's engagement with the Celtic, both in his own history and in that of the Celtic church.

Since you are reading this book, you know that in the last several decades, "Celtic" has been one of several popular spiritual trends. Unfortunately, some of the bestselling books on the subject have had more to do with their writers' romantic imaginations than with the realities of history. The recent popularity of things "Celtic" (which includes the geography and cultures of Northumbria, Ireland, Scotland, the Isle of Man, Wales, Cornwall, and Brittany) is in part an outgrowth of nineteenth-century nationalistic movements and has been greatly dependent upon Scottish material collected by Alexander Carmichael (1832–1912) and published as the *Carmina Gadelica*. In fact the traditions stretch back much farther, emerging from the mists of pre-history.

Celtic Christianity was neither insular nor unconnected to Rome which brought it to Britain, probably in the late first century CE, via the Roman Legions. (See W. H. Auden's poem "Roman Wall Blues.") In

Carthage, Tertullian mentions Britain about 208 CE. Tellingly, although written sources for its beginnings are scant, our earliest are in Latin. The Celtic church flourished in the "early Medieval Period" (fifth century to ca. 1000 CE), especially in what historian Nora Chadwick called "the age of the saints," late fifth through late seventh centuries. It continued into the Norman period which brought European patterns of church life and organization to parts of the "British Isles." But the ancient, "pagan aspects" of Celtic spirituality never completely died out, perhaps because when Gregory the Great sent missionaries to Britain they were charged to incorporate rather than to eradicate. As contemporary Welsh poet Ruth Bidgood writes in her play about St. Bridget, "here in the Celtic lands, the new faith dealt gently with the old. Sometimes it twined about the primitive stones, encircling them with the name of Christ and the mark of his cross."[1]

Happily Dr. Weis makes it clear that Merton understood that the Celtic church was always in communion with Rome. Much more than is historically justifiable has been made of the "schism" (it wasn't) of the Synod of Whitby in 664 CE. Roman "orthodoxy" was not "imposed" on the Celtic church because, while it had always been on the boundaries, it was never outside the Roman church. Of the Celtic church Merton's friend and correspondent, Professor Nora Chadwick, wrote that it accepted *simper, ubique, ab omnibus,* "that which is worthy of belief."[2]

Readers of Merton will recognize in what Weis' book so convincingly demonstrates characterizes Celtic spirituality matters of primary concern to Merton: its affinity with the desert Christians of the fourth century (about which Merton wrote in his collection of their sayings, *Wisdom of the Desert*); its monastic focus and thus profoundly scriptural orientation; its interest in pilgrimage and poetry, and its affinity for place, and for the natural world. Like the church's Greek Fathers (some of whom Weis cites), the Celtic Christians understood that, as God's creation, the natural world was "indwelt" (to modify a term coined by Gerard Manley Hopkins) by divine energies, thus a place to encounter God. A scholar of literature and landscape, Weis is fully prepared to explicate this aspect of Merton's interest in the Celtic. And her wide ranging references to literature and music (Weis is herself an accomplished musician) enrich our understanding and delight.

1. Bidgood, "Hymn to San Ffraid," 6.

2. Chadwick, *The Age of the Saints*, 126. A full and excellent treatment of the Synod of Whitby is Ward, *A True Easter*.

Merton's interest in the Celtic began as an interest in his own Welsh roots and demonstrates Thomas O'Loughlin's dictum that "we know better where we are today if we know our place's . . . past."[3] It ended, as Weis' last chapter so eloquently demonstrates, by bringing together many streams of Merton's interests in the last years of his life. Weis shows us how his wide-ranging explorations in the Celtic tradition illuminated Merton's True Self, how as John J. O Riordain, CSsR puts it: "To the mill of a Gospel-soaked imagination, all is grist."[4]

This is a wonderful book and an important contribution not only to Merton studies, but to the wider understanding of Celtic spirituality. Weis incorporates an impressive variety of Celtic source material and the full range of Merton's published writings as well as his working, holographic notebooks. The book is winsomely written and holds in creative tension what we intuit about the Celtic spirit and what we can know historically about the Celtic church. It is no small accomplishment to hold together spiritual vision and historical reality, but this book does it beautifully.

—Bonnie B. Thurston

3. O'Loughlin, *Journeys on the Edge*, 29.
4. O'Riordain, *The Music of What Happens*, 92.

Acknowledgments

Deep gratitude to Bonnie B. Thurston and Christine M. Bochen who encouraged me to begin this project and then supported me along the way. Special thanks to Bonnie for her gracious suggestions of texts, websites, and videos, and for her willingness to write the foreword. To dear friend and colleague Christine, thanks for offering an encouraging word at just the right time. Ongoing thanks to Patrick F. O'Connell who read an early draft of this book, suggested major organizational changes, and then graciously applied his copyediting expertise—a yeoman task.

I continue to be grateful to the Sisters of St. Joseph who, in my first year of retirement from college teaching, allowed me the uninterrupted time to research and write this book, and I am indebted to Deborah Dooley, former Dean of Nazareth College, who found me an available office in which to spread out my books, notes, and multiple drafts. Lasting gratitude goes also to the members of the Shannon Fellowship Committee for a 2014–15 Shannon Fellowship that enabled me to spend time in the Merton Archives at Bellarmine University and steep myself in Merton's notebooks and tapes of his conferences to the novices. And, of course, no scholarly project could move forward without the expertise and kindness of Paul M. Pearson, Director and Archivist and Mark C. Meade, Assistant Director of The Merton Center, Bellarmine University, Louisville, KY. Their willingness to find folders of holographic notes and unpublished letters, as well as their keen ability to decipher miniscule handwriting made this research project a joy.

Special thanks to Liliana Palumbo, English department secretary for her frequent photocopying, printing, and mailing. No request seemed trivial or inconvenient for her. A hearty salute to Angelika Garrabrant (Angie) student worker *par excellence* for counting words for quotation permissions.

And finally, a nod of thanks to Nancy Hawkins, IHM for sharing her carefully researched lecture on Celtic history and spirituality and to Mary Van Houten whose experience at Iona Abbey expanded my knowledge of Celtic household rituals.

Introduction

One need only interject the word "Celtic" or "Celtic spirituality" into a conversation, and someone is sure to mention that he/she has been to a workshop or retreat on Celtic spirituality, and isn't it wonderful that we are rediscovering this ancient approach that is so needed in today's world. This viewpoint about Celtic spirituality is what British academic and theologian Ian Bradley sadly refers to as its "exotic and peripheral appeal" too often grounded in New Age ideals.[1]

Interest in all things Celtic has enjoyed a renaissance for the last forty years with writings of twentieth-century scholars and historians such as Nora Chadwick, Robin Flower, Dom Louis Gougaud, John Ryan, Esther de Waal, and popular practitioners such as Thomas Cahill, John Phillip Newell, John O'Donohue, and John Bell. Pilgrimages to Iona are ongoing; various workshops, retreats, and short courses are often scheduled at colleges, monasteries, and houses of prayer. Each presentation, no doubt, has its own special angle on this expression of Christianity, some valid and some merely nostalgic or fashionable, but if there is one common characteristic of Celtic culture—whether in Brittany, Northumberland, Scotland, Ireland, or Wales—it is the unique Celtic worldview, an *imagination* that fosters a distinctive way of *seeing*.

Not tainted by a later Western neo-Platonic philosophy that regards the material world *here* as less valuable than the separate and distinct spiritual world *there*, a Celtic Christian worldview embraces the unity of the natural and spiritual worlds, centered in Christ. The Divine is simultaneously *there* and *here*, simultaneously remote and immediate, simultaneously transcendent and immanent. This is not a universe of the "elsewhere

---

1. Bradley, *Celtic Christianity*, viii–ix.

God," but of the "everywhere God."[2] Hence, all creation is to be reverenced because it is imbued with Divine Presence. Landscape, for example, in all its variety, reveals the many "faces" of the Divine. Lakes, fields, woods, rocks, mountains are all holy because they come into being through the creative love of the Divinity. They are made of the very "stuff" of God. British poet William Blake, whose theology and writing strongly influenced Thomas Merton, said it succinctly: "For everything that is, is holy . . . He who sees the Infinite in all things sees God."[3]

Ancient and not so ancient authors have different ways of describing this same understanding. Pelagius, the fourth-century theologian and son of a Welsh bard—despite his ostracism by the Roman church for his views on grace—understood that creation itself is good and that the life of God can be glimpsed in it. To his friend Demetrius, he wrote: "Look at the animals roaming the forest: God's spirit dwells within them. Look at the birds flying across the sky: God's spirit dwells within them . . . the presence of God's spirit in all living things is what makes them beautiful; and if we look with God's eyes, nothing on the earth is ugly."[4]

Pope St. Gregory the Great (590–604) wrote that we know God through his energies. Following this same tradition and building on his translation of seventh–century Eastern theologian Maximus the Confessor, the Irish philosopher John Scotus Eriugena (c. 815–c. 877) taught that God created everything not *ex nihilo*, but out of God's own essence, that is, out of God's very life.[5] The world, therefore, is a theophany, a manifestation of God, a belief reiterated through the centuries by mystics such as Hildegard of Bingen, Julian of Norwich, Meister Eckhart, Johann Tauler, and John Ruysbroeck.[6] As early as 1951, Thomas Merton, in *The Ascent to Truth* acknowledged that the "contemplation of God in nature, which the Greek Fathers call *theoria physike* . . . is a positive recognition of God as He is manifested in the essences (*logoi*) of all things." It is a "habit of religious awareness which endows the soul with a kind of intuitive perception of God

---

2. I am indebted to Michael Morewood for these phrases. See his *Praying a New Story*.

3. Blake, "The Marriage of Heaven and Hell" and "There is No Natural Religion," in *The Poetry and Prose of William Blake*, 2.

4. Pelaguis, *Letters of Pelagius*, 8.1.

5. Eriugena's homilies on the Prologue to St. John's Gospel, quoted by Newell, *Listening for the Heartbeat of God*, 35. Eriugena and Pelagius were criticized for a theology considered to be pantheism.

6. Newell, *Listening for the Heartbeat of God*, 35, 38.

as He is reflected in His creation."[7] In the spring of 1961, Merton taught a course for the Trappist novices on Christian Mysticism that included a significant unit on Maximus the Confessor and *theoria physike*.[8]

To be sure, all these theologians and mystics were not just writing whatever came into their minds; rather, they grounded their beliefs and experience in Scripture which also praises the holiness of Creator and creation: "Let everything that breathes praise the Lord," reads Psalm 150.[9] The writer of the Letter to the Hebrews indicates an understanding of this creative and redemptive power of the Son "whom he appointed heir of all things, and through whom he created the worlds. He is the reflection of God's glory and the exact imprint of God's very Being.[10] St. Paul captures this theology of the centrality of Christ as Creator/Redeemer in his well-known hymn in the Letter to the Colossians: "He is the image of the invisible God, the first-born of all creation . . . all things have been created through and for him . . . and in him all things hold together."[11] The editor of the *Celtic Spirituality* volume in the Classics of Western Spirituality series describes the Celtic imagination and way of seeing in more academic terms: "This is a world of eternally immanent incarnate spirit—spirit that transcends the whole universe of being toward the ultimate and eternal perfection of the universe, precisely because it is immanent in the whole of it."[12] A. M. (Donald) Allchin, a scholar of Eastern Orthodox theology and Welsh culture, and a friend of Thomas Merton, put it more simply: "God's presence *makes* the world."[13] The Celts, Allchin writes, had a particular affinity for and understanding of the Trinity and the Incarnation and thus were "profoundly orthodox . . . It is a tradition which holds together the doctrine of creation and the doctrine of redemption with particular clarity and vigour. The relationship of these two doctrines to one another is grounded in a vision of Christ the Word as at once creator of all things as well as their redeemer."[14] Allchin clearly understood the connection between the Greek Fathers and Celtic Christianity.

7. Merton, *Ascent to Truth*, 27.

8. See Merton, *Introduction to Christian Mysticism*, 121–36.

9. Psalm 150, NRSV.

10. Heb 1:2, NRSV.

11. Col 1:15–20, NRSV.

12. Davies, *Celtic Spirituality*, xv.

13. Allchin, *God's Presence*, xii.

14. Ibid., xi.

Sadly, current interest in Celtic thinking is often trendy, faddish, super-ficial, and New Age. A sampling of websites can easily verify this statement. Thomas Merton, however, here as elsewhere, was "ahead of the curve"—not following a trend, but delving into the authentic history and spirituality of the Celts. His extensive reading in Celtic history, culture, and monasti-cism, particularly between 1964 and 1968, reveals not only the breadth of his interest, but also the depth of his scholarship. His primary sources of information about Celtic history and Christianity were Nora Chadwick's *The Age of Saints in the Early Celtic Church* (1961), Robin Flower's *The Irish Tradition* (1947), Dom Louis Gougaud's *Christianity in Celtic Lands* (1932), and Charles Plummer's *Irish Litanies* (1925). Merton's interest in Celtic her-mit poetry led him to the acknowledged experts and their seminal works: Kuno Meyer's *Selections from Ancient Irish Poetry* (1911) and Kenneth H. Jackson's *Early Celtic Nature Poetry* (1935) and *A Celtic Miscellany* (1951). Notations to consult secondary sources were scribbled at page bottoms and on flyleaves in Merton's notebooks, and he was not shy about request-ing books from the Boston College Library or the University of Kentucky Library. His *Working Notebook #48* contains either full reading notes or references to more than fifteen other works on Irish culture or monasticism such as John Ryan, SJ's *Irish Monasticism* (1931), Bertram Colgrave's *Two Lives of St. Cuthbert* (1940), Kathleen Hughes's "The Changing Theory and Practice of Irish Pilgrimage" in *The Journal of Ecclesiastical History* (1960), James Kenney's *The Sources for Early History of Ireland* (1929), Joseph Anderson's *Scotland in Early Christian Times* (1881), H. G. Leask's *Irish Churches and Monastic Buildings* (1955), William Turner's *Irish Teachers in the Carolingian Revival of Learning* (1907), E. G. Bowen's *The Settlements of the Celtic Saints in Wales* (1954), L. Bieler's *Ireland the Harbinger of the Middle Ages* (1963), and Rotha Mary Clay's *The Hermits and Anchorites of England* (1914). And this is just one notebook!

Working with all these sources, Merton was casting his reading net wide to learn and assimilate everything he could about civic and monastic history, intellectual ideas, architecture, saints, and anchorites. This same enthusiasm—some might even call it an obsession—guided Merton in his intellectual expansion. His notes from Robin Flower's *The Irish Tradition* offer an apt example of this enthusiasm and provide an illustration of his transcribing habits. *Working Notebook #48* contains six holographic pages of notes identified at the top as "Robin Flower. *The Irish Tradition*. Oxford 1947" and organized according to chapters and topics just as one might outline a text or take notes from a university lecture.[15] Merton's process is to identify major topics, make a few salient notes, copy out short quotations, add personal comments in parenthesis, and keep a running list in the right margin of page numbers where the original text occurs. He frequently skips lines and/or indents to indicate new points, using underlining to create his own emphases. Perhaps most instructive—and most frustrating—is Merton's habit of cross-referencing authors, and in some cases inserting a page or two of notes from another book he is concurrently reading. One brief illustration of this practice will demonstrate his note-taking process.

Merton's comments on Flower's *The Irish Tradition* is an appropriately indented series of jottings about the origin of Irish vernacular written language and the importance of the "eye witness." After skipping a line, Merton writes "Voyage of Bran" (underlined), then adds a parenthetical note "(see K. Meyer)" with an additional underlined statement: "Bran carried out to sea by a fairy woman—16ff." If he (or we) looked at this edition of Flower's text, we would find the author's discussion of Bran and his sea pilgrimage on pages sixteen and following. On another holographic page in this same *Working Notebook*, Merton copies out several short quotations about the Irish language, one in particular from Flower that captures what he is sensing in the hermit poetry he is concurrently reading: "The extreme concreteness of the Irish way of thought is reflected in the idioms of their language and determines the effect of their literature upon any mind that is at all attuned to distinctions of style . . . a universal quality in Irish lit— sharp and homely brevity of epigrammatic speech eminently calculated for the rapid thrust and return of contentious talk." Underneath, indented and in parenthesis, he adds this qualification: "(spoiled in bad period by 'pedantics of rhetorical expansion') 110." And farther down the page: "'I think it may be claimed that the Irish were naturally Franciscan, Franciscan before St. Francis!' 125."[16] When Merton makes cross-references to several other authors he is also reading, such as Louis Gougaud, John Ryan, and James Kenney, we see a clear indication of his intellectual acumen that can juggle several texts at the same time and discern relationships between and among ideas and authors. He also makes notes to himself in the right margin to read certain pages of a text, presumably aloud, as if he intends to share his outline of the book in a conference with the Trappist novices.

---

15. Merton, *Working Notebook* #48, n.p.

16. Ibid.

While it is clear that Merton was invested in learning deeply and comprehensively about early Celtic civic and monastic traditions, it is noteworthy that current scholars interested in Celtic spirituality have quoted or written at length on Thomas Merton—a convergence of thought that locates Merton in the contemporary scholarly dialogue about Celtic life. Well-known Celtic scholar Esther de Waal, for example, has written extensively on Celtic history, monasticism, and prayer, and never overlooks an opportunity to mention Thomas Merton as exemplifying in his own life some of the best features of Celtic spirituality. De Waal makes a point that, despite the Celtic monastic isolation of the hermit, this isolation was broken in a "thoroughly practical way" through his connection to a community. Merton, too, she notes, despite his extended time in the hermitage, "remained an essential part of the life of his brothers in the monastery of Gethsemani."[17] British theologian Oliver Davies, translator and principal editor of the seminal text *Celtic Spirituality*, has also written on Thomas Merton. In his essay "Thomas Merton and Meister Eckhart," Davies focuses on these two spiritual figures as paradigmatic for their particular centuries because of their way of seeing the "trinitarian dynamic" that "governed the visible and invisible structure of the world in which they lived and were at home."[18] Edward Sellner, recently retired Professor of Pastoral Theology and Spirituality at the College of St. Catherine in Minnesota, dedicated his 1993 *Wisdom of the Celtic Saints* to "Thomas Merton, my guide."[19] Sellner's writing emphasizes the importance of the Celtic soul-friend [*anamchara*] and claims that Merton functions superbly in that role for him, taking as a personal mantra Merton's quotation: "If I can unite *in myself* the thought and devotion of Eastern and Western Christendom, the Greek and the Latin Fathers, the Russians with the Spanish mystics, I can prepare in myself the reunion of divided Christians."[20] Sellner is now studying Eastern traditions, as did Merton, and working on a book on how Zen Buddhism changed Jack Kerouac and Thomas Merton. In recent years, Paul M. Pearson has written two fine essays about Merton's interest in Celtic monasticism that piqued my interest in Merton's intensive study of Celtic monasticism.[21]

17. De Waal, *Celtic Way of Prayer*, 113.

18. Davies, "Merton and Eckhart," 15–25.

19. Sellner, *Wisdom of the Celtic Saints*.

20. Merton, *Conjectures*, 21.

21. Pearson, "Merton and the Celtic Monastic Tradition" and "Celtic Monasticism."

This book on Thomas Merton and the Celts, however, will not answer all the questions about Merton's affinity for Celtic spirituality, nor will it be the definitive statement about Merton and Celtic monasticism. Rather, it is intended as an initial examination of Merton's enthusiasm for his Welsh heritage, his reading in Celtic Christianity, and his focus on Irish hermit poetry as a general introduction to his study and knowledge of Celtic monasticism and early Celtic Christian culture. In a June 2, 1964 journal entry, Merton writes: "Reading about Celtic monasticism, the hermits, lyric poets, travelers, etc. A new world that has waited until this time to open up."[22]

To begin looking at this new world opening up, chapter 1 highlights three streams of influence that invigorate Merton's reading and investigation: his Welsh ancestors and his imaginative reference to them in the opening pages of his epic poem *The Geography of Lograire*; his friendship with English theologian A. M. (Donald) Allchin; and his correspondence with Anglo-Saxon and Celtic scholar Nora Chadwick. Chapter 2 provides an overview of early monasticism—eremitism and cenobitism—with special emphasis on Celtic monasticism in the context of the Irish church, which was of particular interest to Merton. Chapter 3 focuses more specifically on the importance of the *Navigatio Sancti Brendani* [*The Voyage of St. Brendan*] in Merton's reading, thinking, and monastic development and looks at his fascination with the *peregrinatio* phenomenon in early Celtic spirituality—namely, the monk's pilgrimage or exile "seeking the place of one's resurrection." This chapter also provides an overview of Merton's only published essay on the topic, "From Pilgrimage to Crusade." Chapter 4 presents a synopsis of the Celts' Trinitarian way of seeing: blending the graces of incarnation and redemption and celebrating the immanence as well as the transcendence of the Divine in landscape, animals, people, and the fine arts. Chapter 5 continues this theme of the immanence of God by looking at both modern Welsh poets whom Merton respected and early Irish hermit poetry that celebrates solitude in the woods—samples of which Merton collected into a small personal anthology. Chapter 6 explores the question: So what? Why was Merton so interested in—some might even accuse him of being hung up on—his Welsh heritage? Why was Merton intrigued by early Celtic spirituality and its relationship to desert monasticism? In what ways were the stories of early Celtic monks a capstone to his research and an inspiration for his own spiritual voyage? In what ways might Irish hermit poetry have affirmed and supported his desire to live as a hermit?

22. Merton, *Dancing in the Water of Life*, 107.

How significant was Celtic monasticism in light of Merton's previous study of Eastern mysticism? What context provided the guideposts for this next spiritual travel? Might we conclude that through this study of the Celts—streams of reading and reflection that converged into a deeper experience of wholeness—Merton achieved a new level of psychological and spiritual wholeness? And finally, how might our knowledge of his interest in Celtic culture and monasticism enrich both our understanding of Thomas Merton's spirituality and our own quest for God?

Author's Note:

Prior to any formal study of Celtic spirituality or monasticism, it is necessary to clarify terms. The words "Celtic" and "Irish" are often used interchangeably in common parlance. Historically, those designated as Celts were ethnolinguistic tribal societies living in Central Europe during the Iron Age. They shared some aspects of language and custom. By 450 BCE some tribes migrated to the British Isles ("Insular Celts"), southern France ("Gauls"), the Iberian Peninsula ("Gallaeci"), and northern Italy ("Golaseccans"). There is evidence of inscriptions in the language known as "Insular Celtic" in the fourth century CE, although the language obviously was spoken much earlier. The Celtic written literary tradition begins with early Irish texts in the eighth century and contributed to Modern English three particular linguistic features, namely, the participle -ing to indicate continuous action, periphrasis or indirect speech, and the naming of places. These linguistic features reflect an aspect of the Celtic worldview which privileges the "holy now-moment," the centrality of imagination and tales, and the value of place.[23] Once the Roman invasion had run its course and Anglo-Saxons commanded the area of what is today central and southern Britain, the Celts were forced to the periphery. Consequently, Insular Celtic—language and customs—flourished in specific geographic areas: Ireland, western and northern Great Britain (that is, the particular areas of Wales, Scotland, Cornwall), the Isle of Man, and Brittany on the coast of France. By the fifth century, because of their separation from the main centers of culture on the European continent, these Insular Celts had created a loose, yet somewhat cohesive oral tradition.[24] Hence, despite the complexity of the

23. For additional information about the Celtic influence on the English language, see the website: triangulations.wordpress.com.

24. See Davies, *Celtic Spirituality*, xx–xxi, 3–7 and 459 n. 1. There is disagreement

history of the notion of "Celticity,"[25] the more appropriate term used in this book is "Celtic," meaning the peoples who share this historical, linguistic, religious and artistic heritage. The term "Irish," "Scottish," or "Welsh" will be used to designate Celts living in a specific geographic area and who over the centuries developed particularities of their own language, dialect, and local customs.

The obvious limitations of an initial foray into Merton's voluminous notes, journal entries, letters, and conferences to the novices invite scholars to continue probing what was capturing Merton's attention during the last four years of his life. There is room here for scholars to explore Merton's newfound knowledge of Celtic history, monastic names and foundations, and the attraction of copying quotations from multiple sources, combining and recombining notes into different formats. There is opportunity for a dissertation on the relationship of the Greek Fathers' writing on God's immanence to similar ideas in Celtic Christianity. There is invitation to focus solely on the differences between Irish and Welsh Christianity, their folk wisdom, and the unique gnomic poetry of Wales. There is material for a treatise about the place of Mary in the Celtic church, not as virgin but as mother, and how this view might be in dialogue with Merton's earlier Marian poems. No single study can approach all of these angles. My hope is that I have lifted the lid on a treasure chest that will release not havoc but ongoing rich testimony to the spiritual depth and legacy of Thomas Merton.

among scholars about the notion of a cohesive Celtic tradition and spirituality. It may be there was a unified oral tradition, but not a cohesive Celtic church.

25. Ibid., 4–7.

————— 1 —————

Welsh Roots, A. M. Allchin,
Nora Chadwick

When readers of Merton hear about his fascination with Celtic monasticism during the last decade of his life, they are often startled. "Really? Where does that come from?" While there is no simple answer to this question, there are three streams of experiences whose confluence in the 1960s significantly influenced Merton's study, thinking, and the Celtic dimension of his monastic spirituality. Each of these streams bears examination. The first stream is his awakened consciousness of his Welsh ancestry; the second is his close friendship with Canon A. M. (Donald) Allchin; the third is his correspondence with Anglo-Saxon and Celtic scholar Nora Chadwick. Each stream of interest alone may not have been powerful enough to capture Merton's full attention, but taken together and overlapping in time, they created a upsurge of attention that merged his reading, thinking, and spiritual longing. Indeed, the convergence of these three streams overflowed into his conferences for the Trappist novices and affirmed his final years of solitude in his hermitage at the monastery of Our Lady of Gethsemani outside Bardstown, Kentucky.

Stream #1: Family Roots

Why Wales? Although Thomas Merton lost his parents early in life, he was enamored of his several-hundred-year-old paternal Welsh heritage and kept contact primarily by letter with his aunts in New Zealand. His mother, Ruth Jenkins Merton, was an American who died of stomach cancer when Tom was only six. His father, Owen Merton, a New Zealander by birth and a painter of some renown, died of a brain tumor when Tom was almost sixteen. Decades earlier, in 1856, his English-speaking Merton ancestors had emigrated from Wales to New Zealand. They were a pioneering band who farmed, founded schools, and became musicians. The Grierson family—who joined in marriage with the Bird family from Cardiff, Wales—arrived in 1857. In 1882 Alfred Merton married Gertrude Hannah Grierson who bore six children: Gwynedd[1] Fanny ("Aunt Gwyn" who later settled in England), John Llewellyn Charles ("Uncle Lyn" who served in World War I), Owen Heathcote Grierson (Tom's father), Agnes Gertrude ("Aunt Kit"), and the twins Beatrice Katharine ("Aunt Ka") and Sybil Mary.[2] Merton's grandmother was a Grierson "born in Wales of a Scotch father and Welsh mother, the Birds."[3] It was to this "granny" that Merton's baby book, kept by his mother Ruth, is dedicated.[4]

Granny Gertrude Hannah Grierson Merton and her daughter (Aunt Kit) visited Flushing, Long Island in 1919 for several weeks when Merton was four years old and later, so Tom says, bought the house in Christchurch to keep the family together.[5] It was this granny who taught young Merton the Lord's Prayer and the names of the constellations in the night sky—a reminder, she said, that if he ever felt lonely, he should look up at the stars and remember that they were shining down on both of them.[6]

When thirteen-year old Tom was in school at Ripley Court, England, he spent holidays either with "Aunt Maud" (actually his grandmother's sister and therefore his great-aunt) and Uncle Ben, or with Aunt Gwyn Merton Trier (his father's sister). There he enjoyed the company of cousins and the imaginative adventures of summer playmates.[7] But in general, Merton did not often see this part of his family. He did, however, have sporadic correspondence with Aunt Gwyn and with Aunt Ka who visited him in 1922 in Douglaston, Long Island, and more connection with Aunt Kit who visited him twice—once in 1919 in Flushing, New York and again at the monastery in Gethsemani in 1961 when she was returning from a trip to England

---

1 Gwynedd, besides being a first name, is an area in northwest Wales named after the old Kingdom of Gwynedd; it is also the designation for a preserved county, covering the geographic area of Gwynedd and the Isle of Anglesey and sometimes the term for all of North Wales which is the home of the University of Bangor and Mount Snowdon celebrated in William Wordsworth's autobiographical poem, *The Prelude.*

2. Mott, *Seven Mountains,* 10–11.

3. Merton, *Turning Toward the World,* 177.

4. Merton, *Tom's Book,* n.p.

5. Merton, *Turning Toward the World,* 177.

6. Mott, *Seven Mountains,* 18.

7. Ibid., 48.

via New York City.[8] Nevertheless, Merton regularly sent them copies of his new books published in those years [e.g., *The Way of Chuang Tzu*, *Mystics and Zen Masters*, *Conjectures of a Guilty Bystander*] as well as articles he thought would be of interest.

Although there was not much physical contact with the Welsh-New Zealand relatives, Merton revered his Great Aunt Maud from his visits to her while a school boy in England. Later, at Columbia University—a year after Aunt Maud had died—Merton wrote in his unpublished novel, *The Straits of Dover*, that the Hindu monk, Bramachari—who was in the United States for the World Congress of Religions and who had counseled Merton to steep himself in his own Western Christian tradition—reminded him of his Aunt Maud. How odd. As Merton scholar William H. Shannon notes in *Silent Lamp*, Aunt Maud was "tall, thin and white-haired"; Bramachari was "small, dark and wore a turban." Yet Merton saw in Bramachari's smile and laughter Aunt Maud's smile and laughter. Shannon speculates about this resemblance: "Was the lighthearted innocence and joy in life that the young Merton discovered in the two of them symbolic of similar qualities he felt to be missing from his own life? Was Aunt Maud a symbol of an innocence, simplicity, and goodness he had lost, and Bramachari a symbol of these same qualities he was beginning to believe he could regain through a life of discipline and prayer?"[9] Perhaps so. Nevertheless, meeting Bramachari provided yet another opportunity for Merton to reconnect with his Welsh heritage—at least in his imagination.

During his 1961 visit with Aunt Kit—the first face-to-face contact with his New Zealand relatives in many years—Merton comments in his journal about their common ancestral genes and physical configuration: "It is from the Bird family [his grandmother's maternal lineage] that comes our face—the one Father had and I have and Kit has and Dick Trier has. The look, the grin, the brow."[10] In a more developed passage about this same visit, recounted in *Conjectures of a Guilty Bystander*, Merton outlines the family tree, and in addition to acknowledging the Bird physical resemblance, admits: "It is the Welsh in me that counts: that is what does strange things, and writes the books, and drives me into the woods. Thank God for the Welsh in me, and for all those Birds, those Celts . . ."[11] Merton's jour-

---

8. See Merton, *Road to Joy*, 59–82.

9. Shannon, *Silent Lamp*, 90–91.

10. Merton, *Turning Toward the World*, 177.

11. Merton, *Conjectures*, 200–201.

nal entry for November 5 is revealing: "Sad to see Aunt Kit go. Forty-two years since I last saw her and will probably never see her again. The only blood relation I had seen for twenty years. Lots of lines in her face but much animation. Thin and energetic, she reminds me of Aunt Maud."[12] Clearly Great-Aunt Maud held a special place in Merton's heart.

Although they did not meet again, Merton confided in a letter to Aunt Kit dated May 27, 1964 that he was reading "about hermits and recluses in early Celtic Christianity" and that, because of their Welsh background, "we all have some of this in our blood." As for Aunt Kit's concerns that "social and communal religion" was becoming "a bit formalistic," Merton tried to reassure her that "religion is not a matter of extraordinary spiritual experiences and that rot. The most important thing is a really simple and solid living faith."[13] And to Aunt Beatrice (Aunt Ka), Merton also mentioned he was working on Celtic monastic history—and now that he was fifty years old, he would "perhaps write a book."[14]

On November 3, 1966, Aunt Gwynedd Merton Trier sent Tom two old letters written by his father Owen to an artist friend in New Zealand, an action that rekindled interest in his father's work and a desire to locate his paintings, and perhaps organize an exhibition.[15] At Merton's request, the New Zealand relatives sent various "early letters, clippings about Owen's exhibitions and about his death," as well as information about the family—all of which piqued Merton's interest in his father's art and his Welsh lineage.[16] Contact with the family apparently ceased not long after the startling news of Aunt Kit's tragic death at age seventy-nine in the April 10, 1968 shipwreck of the ferry *Wahine* in a storm between the two major islands of New Zealand.

This was Merton's second relative lost at sea. On April 17, 1943, his brother John Paul, having joined the Royal Canadian Air Force, was reported missing in action. His plane, with four other airmen, went down over

12. Merton, *Turning Toward the World*, 178.

13. Merton, *Road to Joy*, 61–63.

14. Ibid., 64–65.

15. Ibid., 80. Merton edited one of these letters for publication in the Catholic Art Association quarterly (*Good Work*, Spring 1967) as "Sincerity in Art and Life: From a Letter of Owen Merton."

16. Daggy, "Search," 41.

the English Channel, and John Paul, who was severely injured but survived several days in a dingy, was buried at sea on April 19.[17]

Merton's poem to his brother—with visual and aural images of grief—exquisitely reveals the anguish in his heart.[18] Now, some twenty years later, another family tragedy weighed upon his heart. Merton's journal entry for April 28 indicates both his grief and his great reverence for his aunt whose lifeboat had capsized:

> A frightful mess. And in the middle of it all, poor, sweet Aunt Kit, old and without strength to fight the cold, wild sea! I look at the sweater she knitted me to protect me against "the cold" and the whole thing is unbearable . . . the God I believe in is not one who can be "blamed," for it is he who suffers this incomprehensibility in me more than I do myself. But there is a stark absence of all relatedness between the quiet, gentle, unselfish courage of Aunt Kit's life and this dreadful, violent death. What have these waves and currents to do with her? . . . May God grant her peace, light and rest in Christ. My poor dear.[19]

During the next month, Merton heard more about the tragedy[20] from John James Merton, a cousin, and from Aunt Ka. In response to his cousin's letter, Merton wrote:

> Though it does not seem likely, I may some day get a chance to go to the Orient and if I do I will try, if possible, to take in New Zealand and see the family. I should be interested to hear about the investigation of the *Wahine* affair. Though we are all so far apart and some of us have never met, still you are about all the family I have left—with Aunt Gwyn in England, and I do feel that the ties are there. I keep all of you in my prayers.[21]

---

17. Merton, *Seven Storey Mountain*, 402–3.

18. "For My Brother: Reported Missing in Action, 1943" first appeared in *Thirty Poems* and was later reprinted in *The Seven Storey Mountain*, 404.

19. Merton, *Other Side of the Mountain*, 85; also quoted by Allchin, "Can We Do Wales?," 4.

20. One New Zealander, who had noticed the newspaper account of the tragedy, wrote to Merton that she hoped he would be consoled "to know your sister [*sic*] will ever be remembered by those who found her a tower of courage—she walked up & down through the terrified people encouraging & comforting them." Aunt Kit—Agnes Gertrude Merton—had apparently boarded the last lifeboat that subsequently capsized.

21. Merton, *Road to Joy*, 86–87.

Even in tragedy, the desire to connect with "the Welsh in me," albeit the New Zealand version of it, remained strong.

Merton's earlier journal comment that he would probably not see his Aunt Kit again proved to be true. Nonetheless, Merton's focus on Celtic monasticism and his Welsh roots prompted him to suggest in a postcard to his Anglican friend Donald Allchin that they might "do Wales" together in the spring of 1969—an event that sadly did not occur because of yet another tragic death in the Merton clan: Thomas Merton's own accidental death by electrocution at age fifty-three in the Red Cross compound outside Bangkok, Thailand on December 10, 1968.

If, as Merton wrote, "it is the Welsh in me that counts," what characteristics of the people of Wales resonated so with him? Might it be their official bi-lingual society, their distinctive male musical tradition and love of festivals such as St. David's Day on March 1, or their designation as a people and a "land of song"? Might it be their fierce independence and love of country dating from earliest times? Or perhaps it is a certain *hiraeth* or homesickness for the father/motherland, a tugging in the heart for the beloved homeland and its diverse geography of mountains and parks?

Perhaps Merton's work on *The Geography of Lograire*,[22] a prose-poem epic almost completed before his death, offers a window for understanding his fascination with his Welsh blood. Divided into four cantos representing the four points of a compass and playing with the "power of language to reveal and distort reality," the poet uses the voyage motif and the search for a new wholeness to explore the spiritual cost of de-humanization and various violations of global unity.[23] The poem begins with a "Prologue: The Endless Inscription" located first in Wales, which moves to Kentucky with its racism and violence, then acknowledges the power of suffering to achieve eventual peace. As Merton claims in his Author's Note: "In this wide-angle mosaic of poems and dreams I have without scruple mixed what is my own experience with what is almost everybody else's."[24]

Merton's "own experience" is hidden in multiple repetitions of the word Wales. As both outsider and insider, Merton sings his voyage through his Welsh ancestry with an opening question from the wood thrush as the ship's captain signals: "Should they wait?" While describing Wales as "dark Wales," "slow Wales," "holy green Wales," and "father mother Wales," the

22. Merton, *Collected Poems*, 455–609.

23. Shannon, et al., *Thomas Merton Encyclopedia*, 169.

24. Merton, *Collected Poems*, 457.

poet is certain he cannot remain because he finds "Two seas in myself Irish and German / Celt blood." Consequently, he determines to place himself in the woods near the "Stone borders of bards." With Gerard Manley Hopkinsesque alliteration and meter, the poet continues to invoke "Wales all my Wales a ship of green fires / A wall wails wide beside some other sex." He then laments the loss of Tristan, his favorite childhood toy as well as the demise of the family home: "Where was Grandmother with Welsh Birds / My family ancestor the Lieutenant in the hated navy." [Uncle Lyn served in the New Zealand navy during WW I.] With the introduction of the captain of a slave ship selling cargo to Cain and Abel, the poet understands that the idealized past offers no peace and so he must awake to the current tensions of racist America and civil unrest, while at the same time maintaining a belief in love that is ultimately redemptive enough to end all wars.[25]

It would be interesting to interview Merton on his choice to begin *Lograire* in Wales. Why this grounding in Welsh ancestry? A desire to reconnect with his deceased father, his art, his ancestry? Or should the question be: what characteristics of Welsh Christianity resonated with Merton in his last years in the monastery? What features of early Celtic Christianity— which was practiced in Ireland, Brittany, Cornwall, Gaul, Northumberland, Scotland, as well as Wales—were being absorbed into his contemplative prayer experience that affirmed his decision to love and serve God as a hermit? Perhaps the answer is as simple as Merton's November postcard from New Delhi to his friend Donald Allchin in which he merely writes: "I am now trying to get permission to return via England in May. Can we do Wales then?"[26]

25. Ibid., 459–62.
26. Merton, *Hidden Ground of Love*, 31.

Figure 01: Merton Family Photo

Standing, from left: John Llewellyn Charles Merton (Lyn), Alfred James Merton, Beatrice Katherine Merton (Ka), Sybil Mary Merton. Seated, from left: Owen Heathcote Grierson Merton, Gertrude Hannah Merton, Agnes Gertrude Stonehewer Merton (Kit), Gwynedd Fanny Merton (Gwyn). [c.1909].

Figure 02: Photo of Thomas Merton by Sibylle Akers

"...the look, the grin, the brow. It is the Welsh in me that counts."
Conjectures of a Guilty Bystander, 200.

Stream #2: The A. M. (Donald) Allchin Connection

Reverend Canon Arthur MacDonald Allchin (1930–2010) was an Angli-can priest, scholar of Eastern Orthodoxy, Canon at Canterbury Cathedral, librarian at Pusey House, Oxford, and honorary professor at the University of Bangor, Wales. His obituary in *The Guardian* notes that he was a "devotee of all things Welsh—its saints, poets, scholars" and author of several books on the Welsh cultural tradition.[27] While on research leave in the United States in 1963, Allchin was introduced to Thomas Merton by Dr. Dale Moody, a professor at Southern Baptist Theological Seminary in Louisville, KY. There was instant rapport between the two men because of their mutu-al interest in East/West dialogue, Russian Orthodox writers, monasticism, and Welsh culture.[28] Their lively correspondence from 1963–1968 reveals Merton's extensive reading in seventeenth-century Anglican divines as well as his new-found love for Welsh poets.[29]

There were two additional visits between Merton and Allchin before the aborted plan to "do Wales": one in April 1967 and a second in April 1968 when together they visited the Shaker community at Pleasant Hill, Kentucky and learned that day of the assassination of Martin Luther King, Jr. Their conversation during these visits, according to Donald Allchin, covered multiple topics, enriching each of these committed Christians by solidifying their friendship. To my knowledge there is no record of their verbal interchange, yet it is reasonable to assume that Allchin was sharing with Merton not only their mutual interest in Russian Orthodox theolo-gians and his own work as editor of *Sobornost*, a journal dedicated to inter-religious dialogue, but also his ongoing study of Welsh poets, as well as his intent to learn the Welsh language and translate the poetry of eighteenth-century Welsh hymnist Ann Griffith.[30]

---

27. *The Guardian*, February 24, 2011. Particular books of Allchin mentioned by the columnist are *Threshold of Light: Prayers and Praises from the Anglican Tradition* (1986) and *Praise Above All: Discovering the Welsh Tradition* (1991) Scott also notes that Allchin will be "best remembered for his desire to put people in touch with one another and for all to experience God" (see www.theguardian.com/world/2011/feb/24/ Donald-allchin-obituary).

28. Shannon, et al., *Thomas Merton Encyclopedia*, 6.

29. See Merton, *Hidden Ground of Love*, 24–31.

30. Allchin wrote two monographs on Griffith: *The Gift of Theology: The Trinitarian Vision of Ann Griffith and Elizabeth of Dijon* (Fairacres, 2005) and "Celtic Christianity, Fact or Fantasy?" based on his March 16, 1993 lecture when he was named honorary professor at the University of Bangor, Wales.

One personal note: in my informal conversations with Donald Allchin at Oakham, England some years ago, I found him excited about my interpretation of Merton's use of the phrase *le point vierge*. In my formal presentation I had been referring to the June 5, 1960 journal entry in which Merton celebrates the dawn chirping of the birds who ask the Father "if it is time to 'be'? And He tells them. 'Yes.' Then they one by one wake and begin to sing."[31] My insight was that Merton had skillfully identified an important difference: the birds do not ask to wake and move around, but to come into being. Using the phrase *le point vierge* (a phrase of Islamic origin) to refer to this moment of daily genesis, Merton also suggests that at every moment the Creator lovingly keeps each of us in being—a teaching of the Eastern church. Allchin exclaimed that my interpretation of *le point vierge* and the birds offers yet another way to appreciate the Celtic worldview, a view that resonated with Merton's interest in early Celtic Christianity and with his reading of Russian Orthodox theology.

So while we can verify that Thomas Merton was beginning to be interested in Welsh— and more broadly Celtic— culture through his contact with Donald Allchin and his family genealogy from Aunt Kit, his serious study of Celtic history and Celtic monasticism flourished in 1964 when he began reading widely and making voluminous notes on the topic. He had already told Aunt Kit that he was reading about Celtic monks and recluses, and hinted to Aunt Ka that he might write a book about Celtic monastic history. Indeed, the Merton Archives at Bellarmine University have several *Working Notebooks* filled with handwritten notes from books that Merton was devouring.[32] In addition to four taped conferences on Celtic monasticism he gave to the novices in 1968, there are more than one hundred eighty handwritten pages of notes from various books that Merton had borrowed from libraries, some from the Irish Studies Collection at Boston College,[33] some through the goodness of artist Victor Hammer's wife,

31. Merton, *Turning Toward the World*, 7.

32. *Working Notebooks* #14 (June 1964), #18 (1966–1967), #24 (November 1966–June 1967), #48 (no date, but presumably 1966), #53 and #54 (1966–1967). Unpublished holographic notebooks, Louisville, KY: Thomas Merton Center.

33. Merton was writing once or twice a month from May 1962 to August 1968 to Brendan Connolly, SJ, the Director of the Boston College Library, sending him copies of various manuscripts for an exhibit, as well as asking for several hard-to-get books on Irish Studies such as Jackson's *Studies in Early Celtic Nature Poetry*, *Martyrology of Oengus* and Plummer's *Gaelic Lives*. Copies of these letters are at The Thomas Merton Center, Bellarmine University, Louisville, KY. See Merton, *School of Charity*, 294–95 for a list of additional book requests and John P. Collins, "The BC Connection," 19–33.

Carolyn, who was an acquisitions librarian at the University of Kentucky,[34] and others suggested by historian Nora Chadwick, with whom Merton was in correspondence from May 1964 through January 1967. Nora Chadwick represents the important third concurrent stream of Merton's attention to Celtic history, specifically monasticism.

Stream #3: The Nora Chadwick Connection

Nora Chadwick (1891–1972) was a noted English medievalist who studied Anglo-Saxon and Old Norse at Cambridge University, and later taught there, receiving honorary degrees from the University of Wales, the National University of Ireland, and the University of St. Andrew. Although she originally focused her research on Russian oral literature and Central Asian languages, she soon became an expert on early Christian Gaul and Celtic Britain, often collaborating with Celtic scholars Myles Dillon and Kenneth H. Jackson.

If one can imagine Merton registering for an independent study course in the States, Nora Chadwick would have been his chosen mentor. Had he been at Cambridge University, not at age seventeen but during his more mature years with his keen interest in the Celts, Chadwick would probably have been assigned as his tutor. In reality this was the informal guidance provided by this noted historian. Using Chadwick's *Poetry and Letters in Early Christian Gaul* for his lectures to the Trappist novices on the lives of Sts. Jerome, Paulinus of Nola, Martin of Tours and Cassian, Merton steeped himself in Chadwick's research into early monasticism. By 1963 he was giving a series of conferences on pre-Benedictine monasticism, speaking to an enlarged audience. The monastery had recently instituted two changes to create greater unity between the two levels of monks and deeper, longer formation: a merged novitiate for the choir novices and the lay brothers, and an additional three years of monastic formation after first profession.[35] Merton's "classroom" was often overflowing with brothers, novices, and

34. In an August 4, 1964 letter to Carolyn Hammer Merton requests Trenholme's *The Story of Iona* (1909), J. Chagnolleau's *Les Isles de l'Amour* (1951), H. G. Leask's *Irish Churches and Monastic Buildings* (1955), W. F. Skene's *Celtic Scotland* vol. 2 (1886), Renan's *La Poésie des Races Celtiques* (1913) J. M. Synge's *The Aran Islands*, E. Waters's *The Anglo Norman Voyage of St. Brendan* (1928). See Scutchfield, and Holbrook, *The Letters of Merton and Victor and Carolyn Hammer*, 194.

35. Merton, *Pre-Benedictine Monasticism*. See Patrick F. O'Connell's introduction, xi–xvi.

newly professed monks who sat in on the sessions. Consequently, Merton's conferences were a significant influence on the spiritual development of numerous monks at Gethsemani during the 1960s.

Some time earlier, Merton had reviewed the page proofs of Eleanor Duckett's *Carolingian Portraits* for the University of Michigan Press. In his journal entry for December 15, 1962, Merton comments on how his friendship with Eleanor, a philologist and medieval historian teaching at Smith, was a gift of growing older, a recognition of the "autumn quality of detachment" that comes with aging, "a sense of being suspended over nothingness and yet in life, of being a fragile thing, a flame that may blow out, and yet burns brightly . . . the gift of life . . . which one must treasure in great fidelity, with a truly pure heart."[36] It was Merton's connection with Eleanor Duckett[37] and at her urging that Merton wrote to Nora Chadwick, whose books on Celtic thought and history he had been reading for some time. During the years of their correspondence (1964–67), Merton was approaching fifty years old, Chadwick was in her seventies.

In addition to using *Poetry and Letters in Early Christian Gaul* to prepare his classes for the novices, Merton read Chadwick's *The Age of Saints in the Early Celtic Church* (originally a series of talks for the 1960 Riddell Memorial Lectures). He commented in a letter to Anglican spiritual guide Etta Gullick that he found Chadwick's work on the Celtic church "especially interesting to me as I really intend now to do something on recluses and the Irish started all that, or so it seems . . ."[38] Two days later Merton actually wrote to Nora Chadwick asking for additional Irish sources to supplement his interest and research in "medieval Recluses." His reverence for Chadwick's work is evident in his compliment that she is so "completely 'in' the monastic movement of our own time (though you may not realize it) for you think just like some of us and have the same longings and joys in monastic solitude of the Celtic type."[39] Merton had written something similar to American marine biologist Rachel Carson the year before—not about Celtic monasticism, but about her seminal work *Silent Spring* that exposed the dangers of DDT—in which, Merton said, she had diagnosed the ills of our

36. Merton, *Turning Toward the World*, 275–76.

37. Five letters from Duckett to Merton and one letter from Merton to Duckett—often with paragraphs in Latin—are extant in the Archives of The Thomas Merton Center, Bellarmine University, Louisville, KY. In Merton's letter to Duckett (December 24, 1962) he shares his enthusiasm for Eriugena, the ninth-century Irish theologian.

38. Merton, *Hidden Ground of Love*, 366.

39. Merton, *School of Charity*, 217–18.

civilization, and was more accurate than she might have realized.[40] In both instances—Celtic monasticism and ecological responsibility—Merton's comment demonstrates his native intelligence, wide reading, and powers of analytic and synthetic thinking.

Despite her own busy scholarly work in Cambridge England, Nora Chadwick apparently did respond to Merton's request for book suggestions and materials on Celtic monasticism, and his August 20, 1964 letter to her was accompanied by some notes he had been putting together on monastic themes, as well as an acknowledgement of his growing interest in the *Navigatio Sancti Brendani* [*The Voyage of St. Brendan*]. Quoting the *Navigatio*, Merton indicated his desire to write a "manifesto of monastic and spiritual reform emanating from the Irish milieux at Treves, etc. in the Ottonian period . . . the theme of the *paradisus claustralis*. The real 'paradise' . . . is not the 'lost island' . . . but the paradise of liturgy which is the island of the birds on which they always spend the Easter season." [41] Merton also confided to Professor Chadwick in this letter that he was reading Adomnán's life of St. Columba, that he kept the *Age of Saints* at his elbow, and that he was sending her his essay on pilgrimage as well as a copy of a letter written by the twelve-century monk, Guigo the Carthusian.[42]

By June of 1965, Merton had expanded his reading in Celtic monastic history to major authors such as Dom Louis Gougaud and Robin Flower, primarily from books on loan from the Irish Studies Collection at Boston College. He comments to Professor Chadwick that he agrees with her positive evaluation of the centrality of Cassian to monasticism and that he has "kept close to him, and of course use[s] him constantly with the novices." Merton also discloses he is pleased that Chadwick likes the finished version of his essay "From Pilgrimage to Crusade" in *Cithara*, and that perhaps it could be the central essay of a book with additional pieces on Irish monasticism.[43] Merton indicates that he hopes to take part in the eremitical life: "In fact I am already half in it now, in the traditional form of the hermitage in the woods close to the monastery. But I still have to come back to the monastery several days during the week to carry on my work. Next year perhaps I will be relieved of this." His letter concludes with a request for prayers "to carry out this venture in the true spirit of the ancient monks,

40. Merton, *Witness to Freedom*, 70–71.

41. Ibid., 228–29.

42. Guigo I, *The Solitary Life*.

43. Merton's essay was later published in *Mystics and Zen Masters* (1967), 91–112.

and with all their faith and simplicity."[44] At the end of this summer, Merton is given permission to live full time in the hermitage.

Almost a year later, Professor Chadwick finds time to answer Merton's letter, affirming his extended time in the hermitage.

> It sounds almost too beautiful to be true, and carries me back in mind more than a millennium. I wish greatly that I was near enough to come to visit you and hear your discourse, but I am sure that would be a serious and unwarrantable intrusion on your peace. It is lovely to think that in this modern world there are still spirits attuned to the contemplative life. When one picks up a modern newspaper one realizes that this is even more necessary now than in the days of Cassian, and my favourite saint, St. Paulinus of Nola.[45]

Her letter goes on to describe a new work she is writing with Professor Myles Dillon of Dublin. In his 1966 "A Midsummer Diary for M," Merton offers a poignant tribute to his Celtic mentor:

> A touching letter came today from Nora Chadwick—this one I really love, though I never actually met her. She is an old retired Cambridge professor in her eighties [sic] and an authority on Celtic monasticism. She is busy writing still, and another old friend, Eleanor Duckett, a prof from Smith, is there with her writing too. All about the old monks. She writes that she is delighted that I am living the same kind of life as the old guys she writes about: that there actually should be something of the sort in the world of today. This is important to me. For she knows what monasticism is, and she respects the *reality* of monastic solitude (not just the ersatz and the institutionalized forms that have survived today) . . . Seeing it through her eyes, I am deeply moved to the meaning of this strange life. Here I am in the middle of it. I know I have not been truly faithful to it in many ways. I have evaded it. Yet who can say what its real demands are other than the one who must meet them? And who knows what were the failures and problems of those forgotten people who actually lived as solitaries in the past? How many of them were lonely, and in love? The stories of the Desert Fathers are full of material about all that![46]

44. Ibid., 282–83.

45. Chadwick, unpublished letter to Merton, May 28, 1966. Louisville, KY: Thomas Merton Center.

46. Merton, *Learning to Love*, 314.

Within a month, Merton replies about his own research and book reviews of works on non-Christian forms of monasticism and spirituality "especially Buddhism and Islam," and his intent to offer Mass on June 22, the feast of St. Paulinus, for Nora Chadwick and Eleanor Duckett. "This at least," writes Merton "a hermit can do to show his friendship and to bring gifts from God to his friends." Almost a formula in his letters to Professor Chadwick, Merton again asks if there is anything new on Celtic monks, and that he is sending her a study on "The Cell."[47] His desire for and love of the life of solitude enables him to comment: "on the whole I see that it is the best life there is. At least for me . . . one feels close to the root of things."[48] Six months later, Merton inquires about the new book by Myles Dillon and Chadwick—not yet published—and adds a personal note about his own eremitical situation: "The woods are as nice as ever but this year I see far fewer deer."[49]

It is clear from Merton's frequent references to his Welsh ancestry, his conversations with his dear friend Donald Allchin, and his correspondence with Nora Chadwick that something new is being birthed. Merton's understandable curiosity about his own lineage is being fed by a Welsh enthusiast who was learning the language and reading the early poetry, and then supplemented by a noted scholar who could provide names, dates, and trends—something that engaged Merton's capacious mind and longing heart: a triple invitation to find his way home. The next chapter will look specifically at Nora Chadwick's contribution to Merton's knowledge of Celtic monasticism.

47. Thomas Merton, "The Cell," printed in July 1967 in *Sobornost* 5 (June 1967) 332–38, the journal edited by A. M. Allchin, and later in Merton, *Contemplation in a World of Action*, 265–72.

48. Merton, *School of Charity*, 308. The published version omits Merton's final comment "one feels close to the root of things." See the full correspondence in the Thomas Merton Center, Louisville, KY.

49. Ibid., 326.

2

Eremitic and Cenobitic Monasticism

Although Thomas Merton's interest in Celtic monasticism seemingly occurred in the last four years of his life, Celtic monasticism is not a contemporary phenomenon. It is directly related to the origins of monasticism in third-century Egypt, a movement of holy individuals who chose to live a more austere and solitary life in the desert than was practiced in the cities. The acknowledged master of this eremitic or hermit movement is St. Anthony (251–356) whose biography, written by St. Athanasius, became the standard for holiness for nearly a thousand years, a work that was known to Merton.[1]

During the third and fourth centuries, the number of men and women living as eremites in the desert increased dramatically. Devoting themselves to prayer, work, reading, and spiritual discipline, they often met weekly for Eucharist or counsel. Through the influence of St. Pachomius (286–346),[2] the founder of Egyptian cenobitic or community living, monasticism eventually developed into a new and highly structured form of communal life, becoming essentially villages of solitaries. Pachomius was known to have founded ten monasteries (two of them for women), headed by an abbot and bound by a rule of charity with emphasis on humility and obedience. Here was the seed of the ongoing debate about the value and superiority of the eremitic or the cenobitc lifestyles. Which is the greater monastic vocation: that of the hermit or that of the monk living in community? Which is the ideal? Thomas Merton, acutely aware of this tension in monastic thinking, as well as the tension in his own vocation to greater silence and solitude,

1. Merton used this work in his conferences for the novices. See Merton, *Cassian and the Fathers*, 31–39 and *Pre-Benedictine Monasticism*, 17–24.

2. See Merton, *Cassian and the Fathers*, 39–45 and *Pre-Benedictine Monasticism*, 72–114.

cautioned the young novices at Gethsemani that both forms of monasticism have inherent dangers. The former can fall into rampant "individualism and anarchy," the latter into "excessive organization, totalitarianism, and mechanical routine. In either case, the only remedy is fidelity to grace."[3]

The early cenobitic monks of the fourth and fifth centuries engaged in various works, according to their skills—"tailors, bakers, gardeners, and the rest"—and lived full spiritual lives of prayer, especially recitation of the psalms. They also compiled books of prayers, sermons, and spiritual counsel.[4] Not only were there manuscripts containing the "sayings of the desert fathers," but John Cassian, a Scythian who lived among these hermits for several years, distilled their wisdom into two works written between 412–429, the *Institutes* and the *Conferences,* adapting their Eastern ideas to southern Gaul "with a great sense of balance and prudence."[5] From Cassian's *Conferences* we learn the necessity of ongoing awareness of God and purity of heart that leads to union with God. Much of Cassian's counsel reflects the earlier teaching of Evagrius of Pontus (345–399), an intellectual who had collected the wisdom of the early monks into a system of mystical theology that became the foundation of future spiritual teaching. It is Evagrius whose ideas about natural contemplation (*theoria physike*) remind us that through an awareness of the sacramentality of the universe humans can have "an intuition of the Creator in His Creation."[6]

Monastic fever spread from Egypt to Palestine and Syria. During the fourth century, Basil the Great, one of the Cappadocian Fathers of the church, visited these monks. Through his influence, Basil redefined asceticism more broadly as service and charity to the neighbor.[7] As historian David Knowles points out, in one hundred years monastic life had developed all the essentials: the hermits of Egypt, the institute or communal life of Pachomius, the charitable works of Basil, plus "the main lines of a mystical theology" of Evagrius and Cassian.[8]

---

3. In Merton's conferences to the novices, he discusses this transition, subtly revealing his own desire for more solitude in the hermit life. See Merton, *Cassian and the Fathers,* 39, 44–45.

4. For an overview of monasticism, see Knowles, *Christian Monasticism,* 9–24.

5. Merton, *Pre-Benedictine Monasticism,* 41.

6. Merton, *Cassian and the Fathers,* 94.

7. Ibid., 45–51 and *Pre-Benedictine Monasticism,* 123–25.

8. Knowles, *Christian Monasticism,* 22.

Monasticism spread rapidly, via Athanasius, to Rome, Milan, Trier, and North Africa. Athanasius's *Life of Anthony* became a spiritual classic and was read widely. Moving west, the monastic spirit found its way to southern Gaul (Lérins, Ligu99 and Marseille) and then to Marmoutier, western Gaul, Cornwall, Wales, and Ireland.[9] It is this Celtic expression of monasticism (and its connection to Egyptian and Syrian monasticism) that particularly interested Thomas Merton.

In fourth and fifth-century Cornwall, Wales, and Ireland, this unique form of eremitic life expanded swiftly, becoming "the ruling element not only in the church but in society. In a land where cities and towns did not exist, and where the social units were the clan and tribe, monasticism when it captured the enthusiasm of a convert population rapidly became an epidemic."[10] Once a tribal king converted to Christianity, he and his whole clan—potentially several thousand people—often became monks. Some monasteries were originally privately-owned churches (*co-arbship*) given by a tribal chief to a local "saint," a practice that further helped spread Celtic monasticism. Celtic Christianity was essentially monastic, and names of Celtic monks, abbots, and abbesses during the founding years and subsequent centuries are still held in reverence: Saints Columba,[11] Aidan, Columbanus, Brigid, Kevin, Ita, Brendan, Cuthbert, and David. Ruins of bee-hive cells—for example Sceilg Mhichil (Skellig Michael) off the coast of County Kerry—and outbuildings of large, self-sufficient monasteries can be seen today scattered throughout southern Ireland, Wales, and Scotland where the influence of Egyptian monasticism was strong.

The Celtic church—with its multiple anchorites and monasteries governed by abbots and abbesses—flourished. During the sixth century, called by historian Nora Chadwick "The Golden Age of Celtic Monasticism,"[12] there were well-established monasteries at Bangor, Derry, Durrow, Kildare, Clonfert, Lismore, and Kells. These monks embraced poverty, solitude, contemplation and an ascetic discipline which was "austere in the extreme: physical penances . . . such as fasting and immersion in cold water." Often they chose an *anamchara* or soul-mate (Welsh = *periglour*) for spiritual counsel and sacramental absolution, one who sometimes shared a cell with the monk.

9. Ibid., 25–30.

10. Ibid., 31.

11. See poems celebrating several of these saints in Bonnie Bowman Thurston's *Belonging to Borders*.

12. See Chadwick, *Age of Saints*, 61–118.

At the same time—and perhaps paradoxically—"a vivid Latin culture" and "remarkable artistic achievement" arose that puts "Celtic monastic illuminations and metalwork among the masterpieces of art-history." [13] Despite this Eastern influence, argues David Knowles, the *spirit* of the Celtic monks was far different from that of their Egyptian models, primarily because of their deep-seated pre-Christian belief in the unity of matter and spirit, their incorporation of druidic elements into their celebrations, and their "predilection for exile (*peregrinatio*) as a form of renunciation, by which monks took to foreign lands the Christian faith and the monastic life."[14] Quoting at length from Whitley Stokes' *Lives of the Saints* (1890), Celtic scholar Robin Flower illustrates how Abraham's call from God, recorded in Genesis 12:1, to leave his homeland and go to the land which God would show him is the model of perfect pilgrimage and rationale for *peregrinatio*.[15] Merton copied several sections of this text into his *Working Notebook #18*, presumably for his own information and sharing with the novices:

> Abraham—the prototype of perfect monastic pilgrimage. His exile "is a duty for his sons after him, that is, for all the faithful . . . to leave their soil and their land, their wealth & their worldly joy for the sake of the Lord of the elements & go into perfect exile in imitation of Him."
>
> 3 kinds of exile
>
> 1. merely physical—with no change of life—no reward
>
> 2. merely spiritual—"a man leaves his fatherland in fervor of heart & soul" (remaining to serve others as pastors) "since it is for no carnal cause that they abide in their fatherland, their fervent purpose is counted as pilgrimage for them with the Lord"
>
> 3. both body & soul—"as the twelve apostles & the folk of perfect pilgrimage"[16]

Merton also copied a passage attributed to a seventh-century homily:

13. Knowles, *Christian Monasticism*, 31.
14. Ibid., 32.
15. Flower, *Irish Tradition*, 20–22.
16. Ibid., 21.

Now this is white martyrdom for a man, when for God's sake he parts from everything that he loves, though he suffers fasting and labour thereby. And green martyrdom is when he endures labour in penitence and repentance. And red martyrdom is the submission to the cross and tribulation for Christ's sake.[17]

While originally this *peregrinatio* (white martyrdom—solitary wandering, or self-exile) was intended as a private penitential act to discover the "place of one's resurrection," often by setting sail on the dangerous sea with no predetermined destination, the practice sometimes took on characteristics of penance connected to missionary activity. For example, some historians believe that as a result of a contentious physical dispute over the unauthorized copying of a manuscript, St. Columba was sent by his "soulfriend" St. Molaise into exile which led to the founding of the monastery at Iona (563), an island off the coast of Scotland.[18] With missionary zeal, St. Columbanus left Bangor in northern Ireland and journeyed to Gaul to establish a monastery at Luxeuil (c. 590) then to Switzerland and Bobbio in northern Italy (616) writing a Rule that retained the Celtic emphasis on asceticism. A short time later (634) St. Aidan was sent from Iona to establish the monastery at Lindisfarne off the coast of Northumberland. By the eighth or ninth century, the monastery at Tallaght was producing a martyrology of saints and list of religious maxims which was shared by various monasteries. Merton was very interested in their description of the "monastic ideal," and his *Working Notebook* #48 contains these passages of monastic wisdom: "Be not quick to anger or loud of voice or covetous. Eat not to fullness, be neither niggard nor liar."

> Delight not in food.
> Thy side half-bare
> Half-cold thy bed!
> Thus shall with Christ
> Thy praise be said.

> An abbot of another kindred over thee. Far from thy kin to thy death day. Foreign soil over thee at the way's end. Knowledge, steadfastness, persistence. Silence, humility, chastity, patience. Take not the world's way.[19]

17. Ibid., 19. Merton also copies a reference to this homily as recorded by John Ryan, SJ in *Irish Monasticism*, 197–98.

18. See Merton, *Cassian and the Fathers*, 207 n. 529.

19. Merton, *Working Notebook* #48. Merton is quoting Flower's *The Irish Tradition*,

After the sack of Rome (410) and the arrival of St. Patrick, the culture shifted. St. Patrick did not, as popular lore would have it, bring the Christian faith to Ireland. Celtic monastic Christianity was already flourishing before his arrival. St. Patrick's fifth-century missionary efforts in Northern Ireland introduced an alternative expression of Christianity, based not on monasticism and the authority of the local abbot, but on the Roman model of a hierarchy and diocesan structures. Although Patrick's theology was also Trinitarian and creation-centered, his missionary charge was to introduce Roman organization to Ireland.[20] With it arose a tension over calendars for festival celebrations that was not resolved until one hundred years later at the Synod of Whitby (663/664). Following an interpretation hinted at in Bede's ecclesiastical history, some recent writers view the Synod as a confrontation between an episcopal view of church and local monastic communities such as Iona, Lindisfarne, and Canterbury.[21] Esther de Waal argues that the Synod—which resulted in a uniform date for Easter, style of tonsure, and customs for baptism—was not "cataclysmic, a disastrous confrontation" of opposing forces, as these misinformed writers maintain, but "simply a local council" called by a "politically motivated king [King Oswy] for immediate practical reasons," namely that he, his wife, and his court—whose Christianity had roots in different monastic foundations—could celebrate the great feast of Easter at the same time.[22]

While many of the Celtic churches resisted these changes, with Northumbria, Iona, and Wales clinging to the older tradition for several decades, the Celtic way of seeing God in nature as well as in the Scriptures remained strong in the monasteries and in the Celtic people. Perhaps the greatest exponent of this deeply rooted view was the ninth-century Irish theologian John Scotus Eriugena who, through homilies and writings that echoed the teaching of Pelagius and Evagrius, taught that the world is a theophany of God. Christ, in effect, moves among us in two shoes: nature and Scripture.[23] Sometimes glibly considered as the first literal proponent

---

57–58 who attributes this to Best and Lawlor, *Martyrology of Tallaght*, 110.

20. Chadwick, *Age of Saints*, 12, 20.

21. De Waal, "Fresh Look," 31. De Waal argues in *The Celtic Alternative* that this view was solidified in 1987 by Shirley Toulson and then followed by many others, most notably J. Philip Newell.

22. De Waal, "Fresh Look," 31–32.

23. Newell, *Listening for the Heartbeat of God*, 34.

of "intelligent design,"[24] Eriugena is quoted as saying: "Observe the forms and beauties of sensible things and comprehend the Word of God in them. If you do so, the truth will reveal to you in all such things only He who made them."[25]

On the continent another expression of monasticism was emerging. In the sixth century, St. Benedict of Nursia founded communities of monks in Italy and, as a further development of monasticism and under the influence of Cassian, wrote a Rule with its own sense of balance and moderation. For example, Cassian considered sin not so much a crime as an impediment to living a full Christian life. Subsequently, Benedict's *Rule* became the guiding counsel for countless monastic foundations in the Western world and the basis of the Cistercian monasticism that Thomas Merton followed.

Merton would already have known the key developments of early monasticism from his novitiate training and from writing the history of the Cistercian order in his 1949 book, *The Waters of Siloe*. His purpose in this book, as he says in the Prologue, is to answer the question of who the Trappists are, namely, men called to devote their life to one activity: Love of God and the love of others for God's sake.[26] Chapter 1 of this book is a history of monasticism. It is interesting to note that Merton's historical chronicle is a bit sketchy because he had not yet read widely in early monasticism. He mentions St. Anthony of Egypt, St. Athanasius, Cassian, and St. Pachomius, acknowledging the development of both the eremitic and cenobitic lifestyles, as well as St. Basil's realization that Pachomius's style was "too complex, too noisy, too active."[27] It was St. Benedict's challenge in the next century to transform monasticism to a more balanced life focused on interior asceticism, reduced hours of chanting the Divine Office, and labor in the fields. As Merton notes, Benedict's "influence kept alive the central warmth of peace and unity among men in a world that seemed to be wrestling with the ice of death."[28] Other topics discussed by Merton in this book include the discipline of the Cluny monastery in the tenth century and the eleventh-century experiments of the Carthusians, the reforms of St. Bernard, and the growing "pressure of so many active and

---

24. Colson, "Learning from the Irish"; Moore, "Glory All Around."
25. Moore, "Glory All Around."
26. Merton, *Waters of Siloe*, xix.
27. Ibid., 5.
28. Ibid., 6.

material interests" that caused a decline in the primacy of contemplation.[29] Subsequent chapters take up the reforms of Abbot de Rancé at La Trappe and the later American monastic foundations, as well as a section on the characteristics of Cistercian life.

Although Thomas Merton does not elaborate a discussion of various desert monks in this early work, he must have known about them already, as evidenced by several poems written in the 1940s. His third book of poems, *Figures for an Apocalypse* (1947), includes a poem on "Two Desert Fathers"—St. Jerome and St. Paul the Hermit, whose life Jerome had written.[30] In Section I of the poem Merton invokes Jerome who scolds us with words "loud with fight" that pierce even the gloom of our "classic intellection" and "black unhappiness" like the "lights of an express." In Section II, dedicated to Paul the Hermit, Merton asks how to find the road that leads to this holy man. The answer is that we must "cross the invisible frontier / And come upon your paradise, Father of anchorites, / And your simplicity." A few lines later, Merton envies the hermit's solitude of sitting by his cave near a date palm, enjoying God's presence. Your God, complains Merton, is the "One I hunt and never capture"; yet Paul "Opened His door, and lo, His loneliness invaded you." Surely, Merton's monastic commitment to contemplation and his longing for a more intimate relationship with God were validated by the lives of these early desert dwellers.

Later, in the mid–1950s, when Merton was preparing classes for the novices, he expanded his knowledge of early monasticism by reading the desert fathers and researching extensively pre-Benedictine monasticism from both primary and secondary sources, such as Latin documents on the life and spirituality of St. Pachomius, the Coptic monk, Shenoute, and St. Basil.[31] However, his knowledge of and love for Cassian, which inspired many of his conferences, can be traced back to his Lenten reading when he himself was a novice.[32] Indeed, for Merton, Cassian was a pivotal figure who offered access to the Greek mystical tradition and beyond; reading Cassian, as Columba Stewart, OSB asserts, allowed Merton to "move back

---

29. Ibid., 31.

30. Merton, *Collected Poems*, 165–69.

31. Merton, *Pre-Benedictine Monasticism*, xxvii.

32. Merton, *Search for Solitude*, 38; letter to Nora Chadwick in Merton, *School of Charity*, 282–83.

into Evagrius' thought and forward into later Byzantine mysticism, especially of the Hesychast movement and its Russian descendants."[33]

During his early years as master of novices, Merton taught classes on Cassian—the bridge between the early monasticism of Egypt and the Western monasticism of Benedict. Merton believed that Cassian deserves credit—perhaps more so than Benedict—for adapting Eastern ideas of monasticism to a Western context.[34] His comments on monastic figures reveal his depth of study, precision of thought, and love for the solitary life. Merton was adept at ferreting out seminal texts that had yet to be translated into English and synthesizing their main points. Thus, his well-prepared conferences on monastic life and history were a rich and unique experience for the novices, an experience that could not have been duplicated by their own reading. As Patrick F. O'Connell, the editor of these conferences, observes, Merton's "focus was on formation rather than information."[35]

In the late 1950s Merton set about translating the "sayings of the fathers" which was published as *The Wisdom of the Desert*.[36] Of particular interest to Merton was the "social context of their solitary vocation as a sign of contradiction to the conformism and passivity of secular society (even, or especially, Christian secular society)" and their focus on "spiritual identity and relationships in opposition to a pragmatic individualism and a herd mentality."[37] Merton's interest in Eastern monasticism led him to offer classes to the novices—often with newly professed monks in attendance—on little-known monastic figures such as St. Ammonas, the successor to St. Anthony, and on various Syriac monks such as Theodoret, Aphraat, Ephrem, and Philoxenos. In his research, he encountered the figure of Egeria (or Aetheria as Merton spells it), a female Spanish pilgrim who was just "passing through" the Middle East—in actuality a very extensive pilgrimage.[38] His enthusiasm for her travelogue that describes liturgy in Jerusalem, visits to holy places, and hospitable visits to various monastic settlements is infectious. Merton regards her as "a person of unusual courage, independence, determination, and one who is completely set on fulfilling what she

---

33. Merton, *Cassian and the Fathers*, xi.

34. Merton, *Pre-Benedictine Monasticism*, xxii–xxv.

35. Merton, *Cassian and the Fathers*, xix.

36. For a comparative description of this text and its earlier version, see Shannon, et al., *Thomas Merton Encyclopedia*, 528–29.

37. Ibid., 535–36.

38. Merton, *Pre-Benedictine Monasticism*, 169–87.

conceives to be a demand of grace," with "a holy and insatiable curiosity."[39] Although Egeria is not widely known beyond theological circles or considered an integral part of the history of monasticism, Merton found her fascinating and encourages his novices to read her travel memoirs, to "see monasticism through her eyes . . . innocent eyes that take it all in."[40] Merton was even more enthusiastic about Egeria in his journal notations two months earlier: "I love her. Simplicity, practicality, insatiable curiosity, and tremendous endurance as long as she is riding her mule." And the next day: "Etheria (Egeria, Eucharia)—is my delight . . . She is one of 'my saints' from now on."[41] Patrick F. O'Connell rightly comments in his Introduction to *Pre-Benedictine Monasticism*: "His reading of her *Itinerarium* provided the initial spark for his essay 'From Pilgrimage to Crusade,' along with his growing interest in Celtic monasticism, particularly the tradition of '*Peregrinatio*, or going forth into strange countries' [as] 'a characteristically Irish form of asceticism.'" In his essay, Merton calls Egeria's travelogue "one of the liveliest and most interesting of all written pilgrimages."[42]

It is this link—Egeria and pilgrimage—that further set the stage for Merton's focused research into Celtic monasticism. He was already captivated by his Welsh heritage and discussions of Welsh culture with Donald Allchin. Indeed, for Merton, the time was ripe for more systematic inquiry into Celtic monasticism. This enthusiasm—some might even call it an obsession—guided Merton's intellectual exploration. His notes from Nora Chadwick's *The Age of Saints in the Early Celtic Church* offer an apt example of his engagement.

Merton's *Working Notebook* #48 contains ten holographic pages of notes organized according to Chadwick's chapters as one might dutifully outline a text for later study.[43] His process is to identify chapter headings, make a few salient notes, write out short quotations, and keep a running list in the right margin of page numbers where the original text occurs. He frequently skips lines and/or indents to indicate new points. Perhaps most instructive—and most frustrating—is Merton's habit of cross-referencing

39. Ibid., 172.

40. Tape 99.4 (February 2, 1964).

41. Merton, *Dancing in the Water of Life*, 43.

42. Merton, *Pre-Benedictine Monasticism*, xxxi; Merton's essay, "From Pilgrimage to Crusade" originally appeared in *Cithara* (November 1964) and in *Mystics and Zen Masters*, 91–112 and in *Thomas Merton: Selected Essays*, 185–204.

43. Merton, *Working Notebook* #48, n.p.

authors, and in some cases inserting a page or two of notes from another book he is concurrently reading. Here is one illustration of this practice: on the first page of his notes, because Chadwick has mentioned Sts. Bede and Aidan, Merton adds: "See Bede, EH III 17, 142–143" which stands for Bede, *Ecclesiastical History*, Book 3, chapter 17, pages 142–43. Another example: after a section on page two of Merton's handwritten notes identifying three hypotheses of how Eastern monasticism reached Ireland, Merton draws an arrow to a reference for Jerome's Epistle #10 to be found in "PL 22, 697." Being well versed in the writings of the Fathers of the church, Merton often makes such cross references to the *Patrologia Latina*, with book and page number, as in this shorthand notation. Not far from this reference, he writes: "See K. Meyer *Learning in Ireland in the 5th cent.*," and later on the same page: "Chas. Plummer *Irish Litanies*—London 1925."

These jottings are a clear indication of Merton's intellectual acumen that can juggle several texts at the same time and discern relationships between ideas and authors. Merton also makes notes to himself in the right-hand margin to read certain pages of Chadwick's text, presumably aloud, as if he intends to share his outline of the book in a conference with the novices. But what is so engaging about this book that Merton tells Nora Chadwick that he keeps "Age of Saints at his elbow"?[44] Perhaps a précis of Chadwick's text and an overview of Merton's notes will suggest an understanding of his commitment to this text.

The Age of Saints in the Early Celtic Church

Chadwick's Lecture I

"The Early Church in the British Isles"[45] is an overview of Bede's history from the late fifth to late seventh centuries, with attention to Celtic communities such as Iona (St. Columba) and Lindisfarne (St. Aidan) whose monks were the guardians of intellectual life, often accepting boys into their schools for training in Latin and Greek. Because of its geographic distance from Rome, Celtic monasticism adapted to the pastoral landscape with abbots as the governing authority and developed some of its own customs, including the celebration of Easter. The fifth century "Church which Patrick is believed to have founded in Ireland was completely Roman in

44. Merton, *School of Charity*, 228–89.
45. Chadwick, *Age of Saints*, 1–61.

character and episcopal in government."[46] The Celtic church, on the other hand, owes its strength to an infusion of Eastern influence, via Gaul and northern Spain—as evidenced by illuminations on Eastern manuscripts and crosses—a Christianity that emphasized contemplation, asceticism and intellectual activity, especially book production.[47]

Merton's Notes on Lecture I

What catches Merton's eye while reading this first chapter of Chadwick's work and becomes translated into notes is background information about Bede and "the Northumbria created by St. Aiden & St. Cuthbert & the early Church of Lindisfarne," as well as the Celtic church which preceded Patrick's arrival in Ireland. Merton then adds Chadwick's rationale for her book on the Celts that appears on page two of her text:

> I have chosen it because of its lasting beauty. The Celtic Church of the Age of Saints as we see it in their *gentle way of life*, their austere monastic settlements & their *island retreats*, the *personalities of their saints* & the *traditions of their poetry*, expresses the Christian ideal with a sanctity & a sweetness which have never been surpassed, & perhaps only equaled by the ascetics of the Eastern Deserts [Merton's emphasis].

Merton then cross references the notation on St. Aiden with "see Bede EH III 17, 142–143" (cited above) and then moves on to "Conflicts of 5th cent, the Gauith Church, Monastic & Eastern mysticism" which introduced new values, a cleavage with the West, the ideal of service and the solitary life in God; the three hypotheses of how Eastern monasticism reached Ireland (Eastern travellers, Irish pilgrims, literary works, "or all 3?"), supportive quotations from Meyer's *Learning in Ireland in the Fifth Century* and Plummer's *Irish Litanies*, the concentrated influence of monasticism in the south and Patrick's Christianity in the north, and a "conclusions" list from Chadwick's pages 23–24:

a. Patrick represents the ordinary urban xtianity of Gaul 5th cent. Is totally non-monastic, never mentions monasticism. His *Confession* totally dependent on contemp[orary] continental forms esp. Gallican tradition;

46. Ibid., 20.
47. Ibid., 36.

b. the new & disturbing influence of monasticism;

c. St. Patrick's complaints about obstruction—He is *not* a peregrinus

This list is followed by a comment that the churches Patrick met in Ireland had "*spread like wildfire* because there were no Romans and no cities. *Hence the whole Church became monastic.* And Patrick came to *break it up* & bring in urban & Roman setup!! He came as a representative of the conservative episcopal party!*"* [Merton's emphasis and exclamation points]. Merton also makes some notes on Eastern monasticism and the importance of their books and libraries, as well as their intellectual life and art. He seems to be pulling out of this introductory lecture the key historical events that are reinforced by his supplementary reading in Celtic monasticism, evidenced by frequent cross-references to other historians of Celtic life.

Chadwick's Lecture II

"The Age of Saints in the Celtic Church"[48] This lecture examines the contemplation and asceticism of the Desert Fathers, highlighting terms such as *anamchara* (soul mate; *periglour* in Welsh) and the practice of *co-arbship*, that is, land given by a tribal chief to a local "saint." Most important for Chadwick is that the Celtic church was never outside the doctrinal framework of the Roman church: same faith, same tradition, same hope of Resurrection, completely orthodox.[49] Hence, the Council of Whitby in 663/664 should be seen by scholars as a gathering of colleagues to settle a common date for Easter, not a witch-hunt for heretics. Chadwick also has a quarrel with the eighth-century *Catalogus Sanctorum Hibernale* [Catalogue of Irish Saints] that identifies bishops as "most holy," belonging to the First Order; presbyters as "very holy," belonging to the Second Order; and those dwelling in desert places as "holy," belonging to the Third Order. Chadwick considers these labels "spurious categories," created two hundred years later without an understanding of the centrality of Celtic monasticism.[50]

48. Ibid., 61–118.

49. Ibid., 65.

50. Ibid., 70–73. Chadwick meticulously describes these Orders and then dismisses the validity of the categories as "spurious." The First Order ("most holy") were all bishops connected to Patrick and the Continental church, with one liturgy that included the ministry of women. The Second Order, the "very holy" were presbyters, not bishops, with various liturgies and monastic rules, and no ministrations from women who were separate from monasteries. The Third Order, the "holy," were those dwelling in desert

Unique also to the Celtic church was the practice of three types of pilgrimage or *peregrinatio*: one in which the individual leaves the country in body only; one in which he leaves in "zeal of heart" but not body; and one in which he leaves in body and soul, as did the apostles—a perfect pilgrimage as revealed in this early poem:

> To go to Rome
> Is much trouble, little profit;
> The King [of Heaven] whom thou seekest there,
> Unless thou bring Him with thee, thou wilt not find.[51]

The most extreme penances were associated with *geilt* [plural *gealta*], a word usually referring to a lunatic or madman who often saw visions and then withdrew, similar to the recluses of the Syrian desert and tree dwellers—an influence on the Celts that may have come from any of three sources: strangers from the East; Irishmen returning from foreign pilgrimage; literary material from northern Africa and Spain.[52]

Merton's Notes on Lecture II

Merton is a dutiful scribe about the significance of the *anamchara*, *co-arbship*, total orthodoxy, and Three Orders of Saints. He is interested in the Celtic ideal of "seeking the place of one's resurrection," adding a shorthand quote from Chadwick's page eighty-two with his own underlining for emphasis:

> This form of peregrination not for travel to a famous shrine &
> afterwards to return but a withdrawal from home & kindred even
> from the larger religious community to pass one's life or a period
> of one's life in solitude is one of the most important features of
> Irish asceticism and its *chief legacy to after ages* [my ital. 82].

Merton also notes the "3 grades of pilgrimage [from Old Irish life of Columba c. 1000 AD]" based on the biblical story of Abraham's perfect pilgrimage, and adds the "To go to Rome" poem quoted above which he also later types into his "Anthology of Irish Poetry." Merton is interested in the Rule of Columcille [Little Dove or St. Columba], the Rule of Tallaght, and Religious Discipline: cave dwellings, martyrdom as daily struggle, and

---

places, living on herbs, water, and alms.

51. Ibid., 82–84. Chadwick is quoting from Meyer, *Ancient Poetry*, 100.

52. Ibid., 111.

Iona as an island monastery. He takes notes about the "Codified Penances" for the *geilt* (plural *gealta*) associated with a life of wildness, and records in his characteristic shorthand a few facts about the seventh-century king, Suibhne Geilt, who after a vision of the horrors of battle in 637

> flees from human society to lead a wandering life (as result of hor-
> ror of slaughter), lives in the trees, even said to have grown feath-
> ers & learned to fly—a browser (lives on herbs, etc). Apart from
> legend—he was historically a fanatical recluse. St Moling was his
> *anamchara*. Other boskoi ('Grazers')—St. Fintan & his monks 'ate
> nothing but the herbs of the earth & water' (115).[53]

Having a soul-friend is important for Merton. In another notebook he quotes St. Comgall of Bangor as saying "My soul-friend has died and I am headless, and you too are headless, for a man without a soul-friend is a body without a head."[54] Merton's focus in these notes is on Celtic foundations, names of saints, and the *peregrinatio* phenomenon in the Celtic church. It is easy to infer that Merton might be collecting "ammunition" for his persistent request to live more completely the eremitic life with his own symbolic pilgrimage to a hermitage in the Kentucky woods.

Chadwick's Lecture III

"The Celtic Church and the Roman Order."[55] This lecture focuses on the preliminary events leading up to the Synod of Whitby, 663/664, the resolution of Easter dates according to the Roman calendar, the "hold-out" communities of Northumberland and Wales, and the urgency of the oral texts being written down. Chadwick discusses the "Two Eyes of Ireland," that is, the foundations at Tallaght and Finglas that were engaged in documenting customs and recording oral tradition; the Rule of Columcille, highlighting the three labors of the day—prayer, work, reading—derived from Eastern

53. Although this anecdote is from Chadwick, Kenneth Jackson includes mention of Suibhne Geilt who is commemorated in Welsh elegies and comments that Myrddin, known as the "Wild Man of the Forest" went mad after the Battle of Arfderydd (573), fled to the forest, lived with animals and received the gift of prophecy. The "Old Man" becomes the stock figure in Irish and Welsh elegies. See Jackson, *Studies in Early Celtic Nature Poetry*, 110–21.

54. Merton, *Working Notebook #18*, n.p. This is a holograph notation on the *verso* page of typed notes on Primitive Monasticism added to *Working Notebook #18*.

55. Chadwick, *Age of Saints*, 119–66.

monasticism; several Antiphonaries and saints' biographies, and *Peniten-tials*— books listing penances for a variety of inappropriate and sinful actions. Chadwick argues that the flowering of this literary movement was "inspired directly or indirectly by the Paschal controversy,"[56] and offers as an example of this new burst of literary beauty a ninth-century poem written in the first person that suggests the immediacy of the moment:

> A hedge of trees surrounds me,
> A blackbird's lay sings to me;
> Above my lined booklet
> The trilling birds chant to me.
> In a grey mantle from the top of bushes
> The cuckoo sings:
> Verily—may the Lord shield me—
> Well do I write under the greenwood.[57]

Chadwick comments that one of the great features of Celtic poetry is "the simplicity and integrity of the spiritual elite" which often reveals a "life purified from material desires in simple communion with nature."[58] Widely known is this classic and early example of "Monk and his Pet Cat," which appears in almost every collection of Celtic poetry.[59]

> I and my white Pangur
> Have each his special art:
> His mind is set on hunting mice,
> Mine is upon my special craft.
>
> I love to rest—better than any fame!—
> With close study at my little book;
> White Pangur does not envy me:
> He loves his childish play.
>
> When in our house we two are all alone—
> A tale without tedium!
> We have—sport never-ending!
> Something to exercise our wit . . . .

56. Ibid., 159.

57. Ibid., 160–63; Chadwick cites her source as Meyer, *Ancient Irish Poetry*, 99.

58. Ibid., 165.

59. Robin Flower considers this poem the first example of Irish personal poetry. See Flower, *The Irish* Tradition, 24. In 1953 this poem was included as one of Samuel Barber's ten "Hermit Songs" for voice and piano [translation by W. H. Auden] and premiered at the Library of Congress in 1953 by Leontyne Price with Barber himself at the piano.

He rejoices with quick leaps
When in his sharp claw sticks a mouse:
I too rejoice when I have grasped
A problem difficult and dearly loved.

Tough we are thus at all times,
Neither hinders the other,
Each of us pleased with his own art
Amuses himself alone.

He is master of the work
Which every day he does:
While I am at my own work
To bring difficulty to clearness.

Merton's Notes on Lecture III

What seems to be of primary interest to Merton in this chapter is the struggle between the Celtic church and Rome. He outlines the steps toward Whitby with cross-references to Bede's *History*—which Chadwick believes is a misinterpretation of the events—and lists several points of divergence on the Celtic side of the discussion, some spiritual and some political. He then turns his attention to factors that influenced the literature of Irish monasticism and three principles from the Rule of Columcille: "forgiveness from the heart to everyone; continual prayer for those who trouble thee, fervor in singing the office of the dead as if every faithful departed were a particular friend of thine." He notes the "three lessons in the day: prayer, work & reading," and comments that although some of the most stringent penitentials were "webs spun" in the imagination of the scribe, some valuable literature survives through the *Antiphonary of Bangor*, the *Lives of the Saints*, and the *Records of Pagan Tradition*.

What Merton has learned about Celtic history, literature, and monasticism from all his supplemental reading is reinforced by his careful note-taking from Chadwick's book—the quintessential work on early Celtic life by an author who today is still highly regarded. Concurrently, Merton was reading and taking notes from Dom Louis Gougaud's intellectually challenging *Christianity in Celtic Lands* (1932) on some of these same prime topics: heathen Celts, the first Christians, monasticism, the missionary impulse, controversies, intellectual, cultural, and theological doctrines, liturgy and private devotion, and Christian arts. He would have found overlapping yet new material in Robin Flower's *The Irish Tradition* (1947) which highlights the oral and later written culture, the importance of the monastery at Bangor, Ireland (not Wales), the voyage of Bran, various kings, codices, and famous heroes, as well as marginalia found on manuscripts. In Merton's *Working Notebook* #48, he copies from Flower's work a scribe's jotting that originally appeared on a manuscript of Cassiodorus on the Psalms: "Pleasant is the glint of the sun today upon these margins because it flickers so,"[60] and a poem from another manuscript: "Over my head the woodland wall / Rises: the ousel sings to me; / Above my booklet lined for words / The woodland birds shake out their glee."[61] Merton also cites Flower's contention that the word "Celtic" was a linguistic abuse introduced by the Romantics and actually "unknown by the early Irish!"[62]

In addition to this self-motivated program of academic study, Merton was open to suggestions of new texts. In a May 28, 1966 letter, Nora Chadwick had encouraged him to take a look at Olivier Loyer's book *Les Chrétientés Celtiques* which she had reviewed and found "both learned and simple, and most refreshing."[63] Naturally, Merton secured a copy and reviewed it for Cistercian readers.[64] I think it is interesting that Merton, regarded by many as a man of paradox—for his commitment to Western monasticism and his interest in Eastern mysticism; for his ability to live community life, yet function well as a hermit in the woods; for his talent in both *lectio divina* and praying the scripture of nature—senses the innate paradox of Celtic monasticism. In his review, Merton not only affirms Nora Chadwick's evaluation of the book, but also notes that the "great vitality of Celtic monasticism resulted in apparent contradictions: an ardent love of eremitical solitude was combined with missionary zeal; an ideal of contemplative peace sought expression in penitential pilgrimage, especially by sea; extreme asceticism flourished together with a rich and sophisticated literary and artistic culture."[65] Merton surely understood these contradictions

---

60. Flower, *Irish Tradition*, 42.

61. Ibid., 42.

62. Ibid., 109.

63. Unpublished letter from Nora Chadwick to Thomas Merton, Louisville, KY: Thomas Merton Center.

64. Merton's review was published first in *Collectanea Cisterciensia* 29 (1967) # 140, 78–79 and the following year in *Cistercian Studies* 3.4 (1968) # 189, 119–20.

65. Merton, Review of *Les Chrétientés Celtiques*, by Olivier Loyer (*Cistercian Studies* 3.4) 119.

in his own monastic life and had plans to investigate further St. Brendan's voyage—*Navigatio Sancti Brendani*—not so much for note-taking as for emulation in his own spiritual practice and desire for a contemporary *peregrinatio*. Chapter 3 examines the human phenomenon of journey as context for Merton's fascination with St. Brendan's voyage.

3

The Impulse to Pilgrimage
—The Voyage of St. Brendan

Just as a different way of seeing is characteristic of the ancient Celts, so too is their propensity for pilgrimage—*peregrinatio*—setting off on foot or in a small boat without a goal or destination to "discover the place of one's resurrection." This tendency, however, does not make them an anomaly in the human race, even though this imaginative expression of their humanity is exceptional. Psychologists tell us the journey metaphor is deeply embedded in our human experience, primarily because of our tendency to see events as linear. We start from somewhere at some time and proceed to somewhere else; we choose a destination, then create a program of steps to reach that goal; we reflect on where we have been, where we are, and where we would like to go. It should be no surprise to contemporary adults that the seminal research of cognitive scientists Lakoff and Johnson reaffirmed this commonplace and concluded that our conceptual and communication systems actually depend on the metaphor of "journey."[1] Certainly we have seen this metaphor used in pre-modern literature, for example, in the biblical story of "Exodus," Homer's *Odyssey*, Virgil's *Aeneid*, Dante's *Divine Comedy*, and Chaucer's *Canterbury Tales*. Early Christians were considered pilgrims and followers of "The Way" in imitation of Jesus, and the Qur'an lays out the moral pathways of both good and evil.[2]

On the first page of David Adam's *A Desert in the Ocean*, the author delights in the metaphor of journey and broadly proclaims: "Life is meant to be an adventure . . . God calls us to adventure, to extend ourselves, and to seek new horizons."[3] Huston Smith, in his foreword to Phil Cousineau's

1. Lakoff and Johnson, *Metaphors*.
2. Qur'an, 76:3–5.
3. Adam, *Desert in the Ocean*, 1.

seminal text on pilgrimage as an art, contends that "to set out on pilgrimage is to throw down a challenge to everyday life."[4] In Celtic tradition, the word *trasna* captures some of this challenge and decision-making. *Trasna* is the "crossing place" in the mountain gap that beckons onward into the unknown, while the comfortable and known life is left behind. A poem by Sister Raphael Consedine, a contemporary Australian poet, movingly depicts this moment of poise. In part it reads: "Why not return quietly to the known road? / Why be a pilgrim still? . . . When your star rises deep within, / Trust yourself to its leading. / You will have the light for first steps. / This is Trasna, the crossing place / Choose!"[5] Oral tradition and the lives of the saints provide inspirational stories of similar choosing, of hardships overcome, challenges met, and spiritual rewards gained. Often, the metaphor of "journey" or "pilgrimage" is used to articulate these spiritual developments.

The early Christian Celts, with their unique way of seeing, were certainly mindful of the challenges of living such a life of awareness and spiritual commitment. The Celtic understanding of pilgrimage—or more appropriately "voyage" because of the seas surrounding them on all sides—blends their pre-Christian mythology of the quest with their Christian sensibility of finding an isle of paradise. Tales such as "The Voyage of Bran" (seventh century) "The Voyage of Maeldun" (eighth century) and "The Voyage of St. Brendan" (text from the ninth or tenth century, although probably from an older tradition) feed into the Celts' ethnic sense of romance and the lore of ancient wonder-adventures. Celtic scholar Esther de Waal sums it up perceptively:

> An insatiable questing was part of the Celtic spirit, a longing to see what lay over the horizon, for living close to the sea affects the senses. Adomnán gives a vivid picture of a people who appear nearly amphibious, always coming out of a boat or seeking one, a life where the blowing of the wind in a sail, the loathsome and dangerous creatures of the ocean, were everyday realities. But it was not simply the physical presence of the sea. The sea is a place of liminality, a boundary, a frontier, between two places, and if the search is for the meaning of life, what better place in which to site it? So the sea becomes a place of revelation, a source of wisdom, a medium through which messages come from the "other-world."[6]

4. Smith in Cousineau, *Art of Pilgrimage*, xi.

5. Consedine, "Trasna," 45. There is also a traditional Irish song about *trasna* taught to school children about a rover returning home to Ireland after a voyage.

6. De Waal, *Celtic Way of Prayer*, 180.

These tales of sea voyages, or *immrama*, as de Waal describes them, are a unique literary form "full of vigor, imagination, larger-than-life heroes, popular in pre-Christian Ireland." They are apt illustrations of journey literature, our human search for meaning, and significant "vision literature, the universal quest for a happy 'other-world,' both as old as mankind."[7]

Such adventure tales follow a predictable pattern: a hero, whose birth is often accompanied by portents and miraculous signs in nature, sets off with a chosen crew in a skin-covered or wooden boat (*currach*) as a pilgrim to unknown territory or the Otherworld. He drifts across the sea to a mysterious island or islands in the West where he experiences wondrous events, people, and nature, and after extended adventurous wandering, challenges from the sea and sea creatures and sometimes losses, returns home, perhaps forgiven, but certainly wiser. This pattern creates the archetype for the stages of modern physical and spiritual journeys extensively described by Cousineau in *The Art of Pilgrimage*, namely the longing, the call, the departure, the pilgrim's way, the labyrinth, arrival, and bringing back the boon—that is, the "gift," the "new self-knowledge," the "transformed self."[8] Acknowledging the power and validity of this archetype, de Waal refers to all these various tales of saints as bringers of light in the battle of good and evil, "nowhere more dramatically recounted than in the heroic journey of St. Brendan in *Navigatio Brendani*, or *Voyage of Brendan*."[9]

The life of Brendan found in the *Codex Salmanticensis*, a medieval compilation of lives of the saints, appears in two versions. The first is a hagiographical *Vita* that follows the formula of birth, signs and miracles, founding of churches, attracting disciples and foretelling of his death; the second, the *Navigatio*, is a unique tale embracing both geographical and spiritual levels.[10] Brendan the Navigator, who lived sometime between 480 and 570, is credited with the monastic foundation at Clonfert and purported to have made up to twelve sea-faring trips. In the *Vita*, two voyages are detailed, probably more mythological and symbolic than verifiable. The first voyage is unsuccessful because Brendan and his crew built a boat covered with animal skin, the blood of which makes him unacceptable to reach the "Isle of Paradise." With the counsel of St. Ita, a teacher and quasi-foster

7. Ibid., 179.

8. Cousineau, *Art of Pilgrimage*.

9. De Waal, *Celtic Way of Prayer*, 178–79.

10. Bray, "A Note."

mother to Brendan,[11] he again prays, fasts, receives the approval of his abbot, constructs a wooden *currach* wrapped with cured ox hide and sealed with tar, and with his crew of fourteen men again sets sail into the Atlantic Ocean under the protection of the Trinity.

In the *Navigatio*, Brendan's pilgrimage or *peregrinatio* begins as an adult at Clonfert when he was inspired by a tale of St. Barrind, and involves seven years of wandering as well as tests of faith, courage, and steadfastness. During this time he is received by different monastic communities: some brothers come forth from their cells like bees and share nuts, fruits and the Divine Office with the strangers; others are silent contemplatives, led by St. Ailbe. Of course, Brendan faces endless perils: pillars of crystal, sea monsters who threaten their fragile boat, and an island that heaves and reveals itself as a whale. At last he reaches the Isle of the Blessed where he encounters God in the flora, fauna, and strange inhabitants. When he returns to Ireland—"bringing back the boon"—he is prepared to be of service to the "unfortunate, outcast and widowed." His voyage provides him with the wisdom necessary to be able to serve Christ by showing him a Vision of the next life.[12] The critical lesson Brendan learns is the essence of Celtic Christianity—that all creation is holy and everything is sacred because it is the very outpouring of God's creative love.

Dorothy Ann Bray of McGill University has made the useful distinction for us that the *Vita* is a synthesis of oral and written traditions compiled to promote the glory of Brendan and detail the preparation for his life-work, whereas the *Navigatio* is a literary creation that symbolizes and celebrates the culmination of the saint's career.[13] It is clear from Merton's journal comments and his notebook jottings that it is the *Navigatio* version of Brendan's voyage that he read.[14]

11. See Thurston, *Belonging to Borders*, 9.

12. There are numerous popular versions of Brendan's voyage. See Whitsel, "Voyage Theme."

13. Bray, "A Note," 20.

14. In a May 27, 1964 letter to Brendan Connolly, SJ, Director of the Boston College Library, Merton requests a copy of the *Navigatio* and P. F. Moran's *Acta Sancti Brendani* (Dublin 1872) that he saw referenced in Kenny, *Sources for the Early History of Ireland*, 1:406. In July, he requests from Paul Moynihan and Miss Landreth in the Irish Collections an article by Joseph Dunn, "The Brendan Problem" in *Catholic Historical Review* VI, 1920, p 395 ff [actually vol. 6/4 in January 1921]; Grosjean "Vita Brendani" e col. *Dubl analecta Bollandiana*, 48 (1939). Merton remarks in a July 28, 1964 letter to Connolly that one critic, Joseph Dunn, suggests that the Brendan tale "could have been solace for Columbus seeking 'paradise' because he took one Irish sailor with him."

Because the events and phenomena experienced by Brendan resemble in part the voyages of the earlier Bran and Maeldun, it is difficult to separate fact from folklore. Some interpretations focus on a possible geographical connection with explorations to Iceland or to North America. As recently as 1976, British explorer Tim Severin, with four companions, replicated Brendan's stepping-stone route from Ireland to Newfoundland, a forty-five hundred mile journey, in a leather-covered *currach*.[15] But, of course, "The Voyage of Brendan" is more than a geographical adventure; it exemplifies a literary tradition that admits of multiple levels of psychological and spiritual meaning that were not lost on Merton. Once he came across references to this tale in his Celtic research, Merton was committed to track down a translation of it.

In a journal entry for July 18, 1964, Thomas Merton mentions that he has received a copy of the *Navigatio Sancti Brendani* from Boston College and that he intends to study it as a "Tract on monastic life—the myth of *peregrinatio*, the quest for the impossible island, the earthly paradise the ultimate ideal. As a myth it is, however, filled with a deep truth of its own."[16] It takes Merton only four days to finish the "first reading" with the journal comment: "Interesting monastic vocabulary. The geography—a liturgical mandala?"[17] Might there be in Merton's mind a resemblance between this cyclical liturgical voyage and the spirals and whirls of Celtic design which were purported to encourage contemplation? Was his imagination seeing a connection between the monastic life, vision, and worldview of Brendan and his own monastic experience? Was this "the call" subsequent to his "longing" that would initiate Merton's spiritual journey into deeper contemplation and union with God? Certainly Merton understood the spiritual life to be an adventure, to be always on the cusp of the unknown, to answer a call like Abraham's—to go "to the land I will show you." Years earlier (1953) he had written his famous prayer: "My Lord God, I have no idea where I am going. I do not see the road ahead of me . . ."—a curious, yet profound, anticipatory gloss on his interests of the 1960s.[18] By the next

15. Severin, *Brendan Voyage*. A replica of Severin's boat is part of the Irish history Craggaunowen Project at Quinn, County Clare, Ireland.

16. Merton, *Dancing in the Water of Life*, 128.

17. Ibid., 130.

18. Merton, *Search for Solitude*, 129. In the entry for October 26, 1957 Merton refers to finding the manuscript for *37 Meditations*, most of which he wrote during the winter of 1953 while praying at St. Anne's. These meditations were published in 1958 as *Thoughts in Solitude*. Merton's famous prayer appears on page 83.

week, Merton had apparently been reading background information on early monasticism and concluded that "The *Navigatio* is using Celtic myth as a hook on which to hang a manifesto of spiritual renewal in the monastic life, both eremitical and cenobitic."[19]

The *Navigatio Sancti Brendanis* then becomes not merely an epic adventure of going out and returning with some booty or new wisdom, but an archetypal allegorical tale of various aspects of early monastic life. As Cynthia Bourgeault has argued, Brendan's voyage is "monastic to its core: it is a tale *about* monks, *by* monks, and at least in its original manuscript context, *for* monks."[20] Furthermore, it is a lens through which to examine contemporary monasticism. As multiple pages of handwritten notes reveal, Merton was especially interested in *peregrinatio*—a word associated etymologically with the wandering stars and planets as well as with the ascetic exile of these seafarers.[21] In a set of typed notes from Dom Louis Gougaud's *Christianity in Celtic Lands* Merton records:

> Since martyrdom was not easily available in Ireland, *peregrinatio* was sought either as a *means* to martyrdom or as a *substitute* for martyrdom [Merton's emphasis] . . . There were references to innumerable tombs of "martyrs" in solitude, martyrs in *deserto humati* (Gougaud, 363) perhaps this meant the monks themselves. The perpetual mortification of St. Colmcille [Columba], referred to as his "martyrium." Land given for a monastery is "immolated" (Gougaud, 365) . . . and St. Colmcille, offering himself in peregrination, asked in return three gifts: chastity, wisdom, exile (Gougaud, 365, n).[22]

Merton then lists the three martyrdoms referred to by various authors he has been reading, such as Gougaud and Robin Flower: "1. Dagmartra—Red—martyrdom of blood; 2. Banmartra—White—martyrdom of asceticism and exile (for which Job is the prototype); and 3. Green martyrdom of lay penitents."[23] Again from Flower, he copies out by hand: "Now this

19. Merton, *Dancing in the Water of Life*, 132.

20. Bourgeault, "Monastic Archetype," 111.

21. Adam, *Desert in the Ocean*, 55.

22. Part of *Working Notebook* #18–1966–67 entitled "Primitive Monasticism Celtic Monasticism"—presumably notes for a lecture for his novices taken from Dom Louis Gougaud, *Christianity in Celtic Lands*, 360–65.

23. Flower, *Irish Tradition*, 19–22. See Frederick Buechner's historical novel *Brendan*, 86, in which Bishop Erc tells Brendan there are four kinds of martyrs: red, who shed blood dying for Christ; green who work torments on themselves for their sins; white

is white martyrdom for a man, when for God's sake he parts from everything that he loves, though he suffers fasting & labor thereby. And green martyrdom is when he endures labors in penitence & repentance. And red martyrdom is the submission to the cross & tribulation for Christ's sake"[24] Quoting Flower, he notes that "Abraham [is] the prototype of perfect monastic pilgrimage. His exile is a duty for his heirs after him that is for all the faithful . . . To leave their work & their land, their wealth & their worldly joy for the sake of the Lord of the elements & to go into perfect exile in imitation of him." Merton then lists the three kinds of exile:

1. merely physical— with no change of life—no reward

2. merely spiritual—"a man leaves his fatherland in fervor of heart & soul" (remaining to serve others as pastors) [S]ince it is for no carnal cause that they abide in their fatherland[,] their fervent purpose is counted "as pilgrimage for them with the Lord"

3. both body & soul "as the twelve apostles & the folk of perfect pilgrimage"

Merton concludes this collection of notes with a longer quoted passage in his characteristic shorthand:

> Story of Cormac who came to Bangor far from his home (Leinster) & then wanted to return. St Comgall gave him leave to depart then prays for him. Cormac falls asleep outside monastery on a hill. Sleeps from Prime to None, dreaming of Leinster, sees everything, even becomes King—wakes satiated & wearied—returns to monastery.[25]

Another of Merton's *Working Notebooks* (#14 June 1964) is full of references and reminders of books to read on Irish history, art, tradition, poetry, and saints. He is particularly interested in Kenneth Jackson's *Studies in Early Celtic Nature Poetry* and *A Celtic Miscellany,* as well as Kuno Meyer's *Learning in Ireland in the Fifth Century* and *Selections from Ancient Irish Poetry.*[26]

---

martyrs who voluntarily for love of God go into exile; and blue martyrs who are "*currach* martyrs" with beards of seaweed, barnacled cheeks, and "eyes bleared with salt from scouring the blue storms of the sea for the peace of God."

24. Flower, *Irish Tradition*, 19.

25. Merton, *Working Notebook* #18 quoting Flower, *Irish Tradition*, 22.

26. Additional book titles and authors listed on the back cover are Tao, Eckhart, Japanese Cult of Tranquility, *Topography of Ireland*, *Irish Art*, Life of Columba, *Irish Tradition* (Flower), *Lives of Irish Saints* (Plummer), *Irish Texts* (O'Keefe) Kuno Meyer—several, P.

Because *peregrinatio* is unique to Irish asceticism—a pilgrimage "in search of solitude and exile,"[27] *The Voyage of Brendan* holds special significance for Merton as a model of the quintessential *peregrinatio*. He even creates a section of his notebook devoted to features of Brendan's navigation[28]—a précis or set of "cliff notes" of the eleven chapters of Brendan's story that looks something like this (including a bit of confusion over Sections VI-VII):

> Section I: 1. Barinthus, a monk comes weeping, sings of a monk of his wanting to be a hermit . . . flees to an island, Barinthus hears he has a colony of monks, visits, finds island populated by numerous brothers who escape from their cells like a swarm of bees . . . dwelling separately but united in faith, hope, love . . . come together for meals and prayer . . . eats nuts and fruit . . . monastery a paradise. 2. Travel at night through fog and great light . . . come to beautiful island . . . land promised to saints . . . untouched since beginning of world . . . without hunger or fatigue . . . Christ is light of the island . . . this is paradise where the abbot frequently retires and returns to his brothers with garments fragrant from that place. Section II: Brendan + 14 brothers have a secret council . . . resolve to set out. Section III: they fast in preparation. Section IV: building their boat recalls building the ark . . . solemn entry into the boat in the name of Father, Son, Spirit. Section V: brethren never eat . . . mysterious prophecy. Section VI: cf Stonehenge . . . after 15 days they spread sail and let God take them to isle . . . find . . . boy meets Brendan as his "master" and leads them to an empty town, houses, food—all prepared; [presumably Section VII—but not marked] three arrive late . . . on first island . . . steal because Satan is in him . . . rebuked by B., repents, receives Eucharist and dies happily. Sections VI, VII: 3 groups on island: one predestined to . . . island of smokey mountain 3rd latecomer taken by deamons. Section VIII: they leave the island to go on. Section IX: reach another island with fish in rivers and sheep . . . and celebrate Eucharist on Holy Thursday. Section X: land on an island which moves . . . turns out to be huge fish—Jasconius. Section XI: wooded island . . . go a mile upstream . . . octave of Easter, spring and great tree full of white birds . . . birds are angels who fell with Satan . . . here in exile but see the presence of God and are not with the devils . . . they travel about the earth spiritually but gather here on Sundays and feasts

---

Henry *Irish Art.*

27. Merton, "From Pilgrimage to Crusade," 188.

28. Merton's notes are primarily from Gougaud, *Christianity in Celtic Lands*, 131–33.

... return for Easter liturgy return each year . . . Holy Thursday . . .
each year on same island; Easter vigil—on back of whale, monster,
Jasconius: xmas . . . on another island . . . several explications also
from M. Eliade and symbolism of island + Paul the Hermit several
pp of cross references . . . who else has insight into Brendan story.[29]

There have been several scholarly studies of Brendan's *Navigatio*, partly
because of renewed interest in Celtic culture. Dorothy Bray has been help-
ful in distinguishing the characteristics of the two Brendan tales, the *Vita*
and the *Navigatio*.[30] Cynthia Bourgeault offers us a perceptive look at the
monastic archetypes in the *Navigatio*,[31] and Paul M. Pearson argues convincingly for Celtic monasticism as a metaphor for Merton's own spiritual
journey.[32] Each writer brings to light useful nuances of the Brendan story.
From Bray, we learn that Brendan is the "example of the perfect *peregrinus*,
a chosen saint who attempts to attain not simply a geographical goal, but
a spiritual fulfillment and reward."[33] Bourgeault suggests that monasticism
is the "central organizational principle both thematically and structurally"
in *Navigatio* and that the tension of time and space in the tale is a "hall-
mark of a characteristically monastic orientation towards life." Moreover,
the monastic journey is an "exploration, not just of lands and places, but
of the attempt to live, move and respond to the world out of a transfigured centre."[34] Pearson builds on the work of these scholars, arguing that
"Merton found in Celtic Monasticism and in *The Voyage of St. Brendan*,
in particular, a way of understanding monastic life and his own monastic
life."[35] Following Bourgeault's lead, Pearson supports her useful connection
to Raimon Panikkar's *Blessed Simplicity* in which Panikkar describes nine
sutras or aphorisms that "define an orientation toward life [that is, a way of
seeing] which is peculiarly monastic." The monk is one who sees time as a
dimension of the eternal, who understands human time as flooded with the
eternal, "illuminating it while at the same time introducing a transcendent

29. On the back page of *Working Notebook* #14, in addition to a list of books to be
typed or revised and a schedule of reading projects, Merton notes that be wants to read
the *Navigatio* before Easter 1965. Presumably he intends to use this liturgically structured tale as part of his Paschal prayer preparation.

30. Bray, "A Note," 14–20.

31. Bourgeault, "Monastic Archetype," 109–22.

32. Pearson, "Celtic Monasticism."

33. Bray, "A Note," 17.

34. Bourgeault, "Monastic Archetype," 112–20.

35. Pearson, "Celtic Monasticism," 1.

dimension." [36] Curiously—or perhaps not so curiously—Panikkar's description of monastic *seeing* is a characteristic of the fifth and sixth-century Celts and practiced by these monks, whether or not they actually went on a land or sea *peregrinatio*.

Merton's enthusiasm for the spiritual import of Brendan's voyage is in accord with the views of these contemporary critics and of Nora Chadwick, who remarks that these *immrama* journeys into another dimension are in step with literature throughout the world because "man's chief intellectual preoccupations and speculations are with spiritual adventure . . . the lonely pioneering of the soul." [37]

And "lonely pioneering of the soul" is what Merton is most interested in within this tale by monks about monks that is structured around liturgical prayer, fasting, obedience to the abbot, and the cycles of Christmas and Easter. Brendan spends each Eastertide on the island of sheep and each Christmas season with the monastic community of Ailbe. Moreover, as de Waal and others have pointed out, the numbers forty, three, and seven are symbolic. The travelers' seven-year journey is fulfilled by forty days in the Promised Land of the Saints; they stay on various islands for three days, pray and fast for three days, and on one occasion, the wind dies down after three days. These numbers symbolize a new way of *seeing* or experiencing the "interplay between the temporal and the eternal, the times and place of this world and the divine reality that infuses them." The central question the *Navigatio* raises, says de Waal, borrowing Bourgeault's phrase, is: "How does one live out of a transfigured centre?" [38] And as Merton makes clear in Section II of his essay "From Pilgrimage to Crusade," he is very interested in probing this notion of interlacing the temporal and the eternal. And although he does not use the phrase "live out of a transfigured centre," this is the essential question and challenge of the last years of his monastic life.

Because Ireland is an island, surround by the sea, the hazards of travel are significant. There is geologic evidence that Celtic navigators reached Iceland and Greenland, and mythology—which Merton shares with his novices—that they reached America. [39] Wherever the early Celts found

---

36. Bougeault, "Monastic Archetype," 115–16. See also Pannikar, *Blessed Simplicity*.

37. Chadwick, *Poetry and Prophecy*, 92 quoted by De Waal, *Celtic Way of Prayer*, 228 n. 18.

38. De Waal, *Celtic Way of Prayer*, 182.

39. Merton, Tape #102.3 (May 17, 1964). See also, Sullivan, "In Saint Brendan's Wake."

inhabitants, they often became Christian missionaries, although their primary desire was for voluntary exile. Drawing their inspiration from the Biblical story of Abraham, "the granddaddy" of all pilgrims,[40] the Celtic monks, claims Merton in "From Pilgrimage to Crusade," had a "mystic spirituality . . . built on a charism of pilgrimage and navigation." Their travel was quite different from the traditional pilgrimage which has a geographical goal of a Promised Land in mind; theologically, they were seeking their "place of resurrection . . . It was a journey to a mysterious, unknown, but divinely appointed place, which was to be the place of the monk's ultimate meeting with God."[41]

A few paragraphs later, Merton reinforces this distinction:

> The pilgrimage of the Irish monk was therefore not merely the restless search of an unsatisfied romantic heart. It was a profound and existential tribute to the realities perceived in the very structure of the world, and of man, and of their being: a sense of ontological and spiritual dialogue between man and creation in which spiritual and bodily realities interweave and interlace themselves like manuscript illuminations in the Book of Kells.[42]

The Celtic monk's life often flowered into enormous "spiritual creativity" because "his vocation was to mystery and growth, to liberty and abandonment to God, in self-commitment to the apparent irrationality of the winds and the seas, in witness to the wisdom of God the Father and Lord of the elements."[43] Jessica Powers (1905–88) the Carmelite nun and poet, understood the ramifications of this call not only to Abraham but also to us. In her poem named for this patriarch, she cries out to the "old nomad": "Are you my father? Come to me in pity. / Mine is a far and lonely journey too."[44]

In Merton's scholarly reading, Nora Chadwick's *The Age of Early Celtic Saints* is clearly valuable and provides supportive information for his incisive writing about the phenomenon of Celtic *peregrinatio*—the lure of

---

40. Merton, Tape #41.2 (January 16, 1963). Merton relishes calling Abraham's pilgrimage the "granddaddy of journeys" because "We live on earth as strangers" and "everything about the monastic life is paradox."

41. Merton, "From Pilgrimage to Crusade," 190; Merton, *Mystics and Zen Masters*, 95.

42. Merton, "From Pilgrimage to Crusade," 191; Merton, *Mystics and Zen Masters*, 97.

43. Merton, "From Pilgrimage to Crusade," 192; Merton, *Mystics and Zen Masters*, 97–98.

44. Powers, "Abraham," 66.

travel, its concomitant asceticism, and monastic discipline. In one of his notebooks, Merton underscores Chadwick's praise for this specific contribution of the Celtic church, noting in italics that Celtic *peregrinatio* is "*its chief legacy to after ages.*"[45]

I think it is fair to say that Merton considers himself an inheritor—and guardian—of this Celtic legacy, perhaps even a new Brendan. Surely he understood the history of monasticism, from his own study of the Desert Fathers, his classes for the novices on monasticism, and his translations in *The Wisdom of the Desert* (1960). In addition to his reading widely in early monasticism, Merton was concurrently writing short pieces on solitude and the importance of reinvigorating it within Trappist life, for example, "The Case for a Renewal of Eremitism in the Monastic State"[46] and "The Cell."[47] He understood and was already practicing the chief traits of monasticism: asceticism, recitation of the Divine Office, and personal contemplation. He understood, as David Adam so aptly phrases it in his meditation on Brendan's voyage:

> The desert is not a hiding place but a place where all is revealed. If the desert is a place of pruning, it is a pruning that life may blossom and grow in the right direction. It is not so much a return to the natural as to the supernatural, to discover the extra-ordinary that is ever present in the ordinary. The desert is the place where they sought to live life in the depths and in a constant relationship to the ever-present God. The Celtic Christians withdrew from a world that was blind to the presence and sought to live in the depths and wonder of God.[48]

How moved Merton was in July 1964 reading Adomnán's *Life of Columba* in Latin to discover its poetic richness and acknowledgement of the sacramental power within creation; prophecies and miracles were signs, not of authority, but of life.[49] How happy Merton must have been to come upon the tale of Cormac who went in search of a "desert in the sea."[50] What

---

45. Merton, *Working Notebook #14*.

46. Merton, *Collectanea Cisterciensia*, January 1965 and *Contemplation in a World of Action*, 306–39.

47. Merton published this essay in A. M. Allchin's journal *Sobornost* 5 (June 1967) 332–38; see also Merton, *Contemplation in a World of Action*, 265–72.

48. Adam, *Desert in the Ocean*, 4.

49. Merton, *Dancing in the Water of Life*, 126.

50. Merton, "From Pilgrimage to Crusade," 190 n. 15; no note in the version printed in *Mystics and Zen Masters*.

a fine description of the Celtic *peregrinatio*—monks who lived on the edge of the sea yet were influenced by the spirit of the desert fathers in Egypt and Syria. In the words of David Adam: "Some sought a desert in the ocean so that they could live in the depth of God's presence. By placing themselves on the 'edge' of this world, they sought the chance to let the other world break through and to see both as one."[51] Just the kind of paradox Merton would find intriguing!

As he was going deeper into his own spiritual journey as a Trappist monk, Merton clearly understood the risk of setting out on unknown seas, trusting God to reveal the path. The risk factor embraced by these early Celtic monks is astounding. After all, despite the lure of the sea, extensive travel for ordinary people was not a common activity in this fifth and sixth-century world of small villages and tribal thinking. Travel was dangerous and, as David Adam comments:

> On the sea there is no room for the unaware, there has to be con-stant watching of the wind and waves, a reckoning by the sun and stars. It is important to make sure you are on course and not just drifting with the current. There has to be a constant care of the vessel for on this all life depends. A voyage of discovery is not just a rowing about, it is about being open and aware.[52]

Such travel is "never entered into unadvisedly, lightly or wantonly,"[53] Moreover, such a voyage puts one at the mercy of God. Despite all the sea monsters of Brendan's voyage and whatever one makes of these fantastical tales, we must remember, as Adam reminds us, that "Their pilgrimage is not only 'for the love of God' but *in and into* the love of God."[54] One is easily reminded of the eighth-century Celtic hymn, still sung today, which may well have been a guiding "psalm" for early Celtic wayfarers:

> Be Thou my vision, O Lord of my heart;
> Naught is all else to me save that Thou art.
> Thou my best thought by day and by night;
> Waking or sleeping Thy presence my Light.[55]

---

51. Adam, *Desert in the Ocean*, 4–5.

52. Ibid., 31.

53. Ibid., 55.

54. Ibid., 42, my italics.

55. Translated by Eleanor Hull, 1938 in Marier, *St. Pius X Hymnal*, 21.

Surely, Merton understood the dangers and the necessity of keeping one's eye on God. His own physical pilgrimage—recorded with exquisite detail in his autobiography, *The Seven Storey Mountain*—had brought him from his birthplace in Prades, France to Long Island, Bermuda, St-Antonin, an English public school, Cambridge, Columbia University, St. Bonaventure College, and the monastery at Gethsemani, Kentucky. There began his real spiritual journey, and even though several times in his journal he comments that he has at last found what he was looking for, there were always more physical and spiritual horizons to embrace. On his fiftieth birthday, Merton shares in his journal an insight that is particularly revealing. Although he does not mention Brendan or the *Navigatio*, he clearly has interiorized the essentials of *peregrinatio*:

> Last night, before going to bed, realized momentarily what solitude really means: When the ropes are cast off and the skiff is no longer tied to land, but heads out to sea without ties, without restraints! Not the sea of passion, on the contrary, the sea of purity and love that is without care.[56]

The Voyage of Brendan is a good story, and Merton always loved a good story. After all, he was a writer. Moreover, the stories of these wandering Celts energized Merton's gypsy feet. In his middle years in the monastery, Merton had a dream of relocating with the Carthusians or the Camaldolese, believing that their life, more austere and solitary than the Trappists, was what God was asking of him. "His hunger for ever deeper solitude fueled the temptation to join an order in which he might live the life of a hermit."[57] Both of his abbots, Dom Frederic Dunne and Dom James Fox, offered Merton wise counsel about this restlessness, and in 1948, Dom James allowed Merton space for solitude in the rare book vault and in 1949 gave him permission to go beyond the cloister wall for prayer and contemplation. In January 1953 Merton was allowed to use an abandoned tool shed for solitude which he named St. Anne and where he wrote *Thoughts in Solitude* (1958). Continuing his exploration of the hermit or eremitic life, Merton devoted a chapter to it in *The Silent Life* (1957), in which he argues that the "hermit life rooted in the tradition of the desert fathers has a legitimate place in contemporary monastic life."[58] By 1960, Merton had his eye on a cinder block retreat house planned for Mount Olivet on the monastery

---

56. Merton, *Dancing in the Water of Life*, 200.

57. Shannon, et al., *Thomas Merton Encyclopedia*, 42.

58. Ibid., 41.

grounds, originally intended for ecumenical gatherings; over the next few years, he gained permission to spend time there for prayer, and by August 1965 Merton became a full time hermit at "St. Mary of Carmel." Nevertheless, Merton's ongoing correspondence with Ernesto Cardenal initiated a short-lived desire to join Our Lady of Solentiname, Cardenal's contemplative community in Nicaragua. By 1968 Merton sensed that he was too available in the Kentucky hermitage and began his search for another site in Mexico, California, or Alaska.

Despite these periods of unrest, Merton's ongoing exploration of the history, the saints, and the movements in early Celtic monasticism continued transforming an exterior impulse to pilgrimage into the more important and pervasive inner "lonely pioneering of the soul." His first reaction to reading the *Navigatio Sancti Brendan* is telling: "a liturgical mandala?" Merton immediately realized that this engaging tale is about a new way of seeing, about asceticism and contemplation, about an encounter with God that transcends time and space, and that the essential stance of this "transfigured centre" is to live not only *at* the mercy of God, but also to discover the guiding power of living *in* that mercy. Merton experiences a flash of this insight on December 9, 1964, on his way from the hermitage to the monastery:

> [T]his morning, coming down, seeing the multitude of stars above the bare branches of the wood, I was suddenly hit, as it were, with the whole package of meaning of everything: that the immense mercy of God was upon me, that the Lord in infinite kindness had looked on me and given me this vocation out of love, and that he had always intended this, and how foolish and trivial had been all my fears and twistings and desperation.[59]

Merton's fascination with the *peregrinatio* of Celtic monasticism is reflected in his own monastic pilgrimage and his choice to be a bystander, an exile between this world and the next. As he says in one of his conferences to the novices: By becoming a monk, "one becomes a stranger, an exile . . . we go into the midst of the unknown, we live on earth as strangers."[60] To the last year of his monastic life, Merton's focus on the inner pilgrimage and finding the place of resurrection remained clear. Indeed, it is the expressed focus of his final journey to Asia: "I have left my monastery to come here not just as a research scholar or even as an author. I come as a pilgrim . . .

59. Merton, *Dancing in the Water of Life*, 177–78.

60. Merton, Tape #41.2, (January 16, 1963) quoted by Pearson, "Sentinels," 8.

to drink from ancient sources of monastic vision and experience."[61] As Paul Pearson has so persuasively stated: "Merton's sense of exploring, wandering, homelessness, questioning, strangeness, his continuing conversion, his sense of journeying kept him moving forward like Brendan, like Abraham in search of the Promised Land, in search of his hearts' home, and of his place of resurrection."[62]

And, of course, Merton is not alone in needing this wisdom. Men and women of faith today, both lay, religious, and monastic, are challenged to continue the voyage of Brendan—not a physical *peregrinatio*, but a spiritual pilgrimage that marks them as exiles who are counter-cultural to this topsy-turvy world and seeking to "live out of a transfigured centre"—a Celtic way of seeing and experiencing the transcendence of time and place. That ancient Celtic word *trasna* is pertinent to our contemporary challenges—*trasna*, the "crossing place" or gap between rocks that forces the pilgrim to make a decision to return to safety and the known, or to forge ahead into the potentially scary and dangerous unknown. Pope Francis is credited with commenting: "Life is a journey. When we stop, things don't go right." Similarly, a Buddhist saying captures something of this same quandary: If you are facing in the right direction, all you need to do is keep on walking. Recently, Sister of Charity Ellen Dauwer has written: "These days life in God is one of journey . . . There is neither clear path nor exact destination for daily choices and steps determine the way. The gifts of the Spirit provide light and the grace of God is sustenance . . . pray for an open mind, a discerning spirit, and a loving heart for the days ahead. Who knows what lies before us and what is yet to come!"[63] Indeed, just as Brendan set off into the unknown, we as a church and as individuals also sail uncharted seas, trusting to the great mercy of an "everywhere God."

From Pilgrimage to Crusade

Although Merton was fascinated with early Celtic monasticism and in particular the *peregrinatio* of the monks, he did not, as he hinted to Aunt Ka, write a book about it. Yet because he had steeped himself in the Brendan story and distilled its lessons, Merton was amply prepared to write an essay on the importance of "journey" within the human story. Published first in

61. Merton, *Asian Journal*, 312–13.

62. Pearson, "Sentinels," 13.

63. Dauwer, *Praying*, 6.

Cithara 4.1 (November 1964) 3–21, in *Tomorrow: A Journal of Metaphysics, Cosmology and Traditional Studies* 13.2 (Spring 1965) 90–102, and later in *Mystics and Zen Masters* (1967) 91–112, Merton's essay is, as he writes to Quaker June Yungblut, "central to my thought."[64] Merton had been pondering the journey or pilgrimage motif, both physical and spiritual. He realized, as Patrick O'Connell has so perceptively phrased it in his introduction to Merton's essay, the

> problematic, indeed catastrophic dimensions of such journeys when made under the distorted influence of a faulty anthropology and a defective spirituality, exemplified both in the East during the Crusades and in the West in the conquest of the Americas; and the need to recover an authentic sense of pilgrimage that rediscovers paradise—personal, communal, even cosmic integration—not by driving out "the other" but by recognizing the same humanity, the same divine image, "in the aborigine who most differs from ourselves . . . the stranger who is Christ our fellow-pilgrim and our brother."[65]

The almost twenty-page essay, divided into five sections and complemented by seventy footnotes, immediately establishes the pilgrimage motif as central to human existence—in prehistoric religious cultures, in Jewish pilgrimages, and in Christian salvation history. Each physical pilgrimage is a "symbolic acting out of an inner journey."[66]

Section I

Section I of Merton's essay recounts the journey of Aetheria (more commonly spelled Egeria)—already mentioned in chapter 2—a female pilgrim from Spain who journeyed to Jerusalem, the Egyptian desert, and even to Mount Sinai in the Arabian desert, visiting "colonies of hermits living in huts and caves."[67] Some months earlier, after reading Egeria's travelogue for the first time, Merton had written in his journal:

> I love her. Simplicity, practicality, insatiable curiosity, and tremendous endurance as long as she is riding her mule (laments a little when she has to go "straight up" the side of Sinai—any influence

64. Merton, *Hidden Ground*, 642.

65. O'Connell, introduction to Merton, "From Pilgrimage to Crusade," 185.

66. Merton, "From Pilgrimage to Crusade," 187.

67. Ibid., 186.

on St. John of the Cross? All the holy women she meets—they must have been delighted with her and overwhelmed. This is a really marvelous book, one of the greatest monuments of fourth-century literature, and too few know it . . . Is she Spanish? Sounds like a Spaniard, with the simplicity, mixture of hope, humor, idealism and endurance. Or maybe someday she will turn out to have been Irish![68]

The next day's journal entry reads: " Etheria (Egeria, Eucharia) –is my delight . . . .She is one of 'my saints' from now on."[69] Merton's enthusiasm for this female pilgrim extended even to discussing her in his classes for the novices on pre-Benedictine monasticism. Egeria, he said, is: "a person of unusual courage, independence, determination, and one who is completely set on fulfilling what she conceives to be a demand of grace . . . impelled to visit *all* the holy places . . . She has a holy and insatiable curiosity" traveling "with two guidebooks in hand: not Baedeker, but the *Bible* and the *Onomasticon* of Eusebius in Jerome's Latin translation."[70]

Because Egeria's account of her travels reveals much of the liturgical practices of the time, it is revered as the first record of Easter liturgies and the Paschal Triduum. She notices that the Eucharistic celebrations focused more on the resurrection of Jesus than on his crucifixion, and that the Holy Sepulchre, the site of Jesus' resurrection, was held in more reverence than Calvary, the site of his death. Although Merton's ardor for Egeria cools a bit in the classroom because he is suspicious of the depth of her interior piety, in the final analysis, he finds her "an essential witness giving us a living picture of Palestinian monasticism as she saw it."[71]

Such a revealing piece of travel literature is an "anthropological find" and reminiscent of the writing of American colonist Madame Sarah Kemble Knight who, in 1704, journeyed several months by horseback from Boston to New York City to settle the financial accounts of a deceased relative.[72] Her travelogue brings to light more of the lived culture and biases of her time than do official documents of the struggling Puritan colonies. Indeed, I would argue that accounts from "common folk"—such as Egeria

68. Merton, *Dancing in the Water of Life*, 43.

69. Ibid., 43.

70. Merton, *Pre-Benedictine Monasticism*, 171–72.

71. Ibid., 173, 187.

72. Knight, *Heath Anthology*, 609–26.

and Sarah Kemble Knight—offer essential candid human perspectives on the customs and values of the time.

Section II

This section of "Pilgrimage" highlights the Irish *peregrinatio* or wandering that was part of Celtic asceticism in which the monk or individual set out with no clear destination in mind "but in search of solitude and exile," entrusting the self to God and often to the sea. It is this impulse that led St. Brendan to set off on the sea to find the "place of resurrection." The model for this physical and spiritual pilgrimage is the Hebrew story of Abraham, the quintessential pilgrim, who left "his own country" for the "land which God had shown him, to wit the 'Land of Promise.'"[73] The wandering, or white martyrdom, of the Irish monk was not "aimless wandering for its own sake. It was a journey to a mysterious, unknown, but divinely appointed place, which was to be the place of the monk's ultimate meeting with God."[74] Moreover, as Merton writes, such a journey was not a lark, but "was in profound relationship with an inner experience of *continuity* between the natural and the supernatural, between the sacred and the profane, between this world and the next: a continuity both in time and space. For the Celt, as for archaic and primitive man, the true reality is that which is manifested obscurely and sacramentally in symbol, sacrament, and myth."[75] Merton had high regard for these Celtic pilgrimages as a vocation "to mystery and to growth, to liberty and abandonment to God, in self-commitment to the apparent irrationality of the winds and the seas, in witness to the wisdom of God the Father and Lord of the elements." He regarded them as unique spiritual experiences that overflowed into inner holiness and outer expression in literature: "Better perhaps than the Greeks, some of the Celtic monks arrived at the purity of that *theoria physike* which sees God not in the essences or *logoi* of things, but in a hierophanic cosmos; hence the marvelous vernacular nature poetry of the sixth and seventh-century Celtic hermits."[76]

In hindsight, one can view Merton's 1968 pilgrimage to Asia as such a mysterious and divinely appointed journey. Looking at the great Buddhas

73. Merton, "From Pilgrimage to Crusade," 189, quoting Chadwick, *Age of Saints*, 83.

74. Ibid., 190.

75. Ibid., 191.

76. Ibid., 192.

at Polonnaruwa, Merton "was suddenly, almost forcibly jerked clean out of the habitual, half-tied vision of things, and an inner clearness, clarity, as if exploding from the rocks themselves, became evident and obvious . . . I know and have seen what I was obscurely looking for . . . have got beyond the shadow and the disguise."[77] And, indeed, a few days later, December 10, 1968, Merton did find the "place of his resurrection." From another perspective, one could say that the Risen One found him.

Section III

The third section of Merton's essay offers an insight into the historical Celtic influence on penance or asceticism from the sixth to the eleventh centuries—a kind of inner spiritual journey that often took the form of holy exile for the penitent. Originally, penance for serious sin was completed only once and in a public place. By the eighth century penitence had become more private and could be repeated as needed or commanded. The sinner might be sent into exile for a stated duration or sent to a particular bishop on the continent to *receive* a penance; once he had completed the terms of his penance and returned to Ireland, he would be absolved from his sin. Gradually offenses were "systematized" so that many little offenses could result in the assignment of a pilgrimage to any of the major Christian sites (Jerusalem, Rome, Canterbury, Compostela) or minor ones (LePuy, St. Gilles, Rocamadour). After such wandering, the penitent often returned to a cloister where the commitment to stability offered the opportunity for a spiritual pilgrimage. Merton comments that, generally, the "holy exile," who was wearing distinctive garb and a badge, was recognized as a sacred person to be treated with respect, fed, and protected. Paradoxically, he was an outcast with a privileged place in the church.

Human nature, however, given to excesses and mischief, prompted some sinners to band together as bandits, robbers, and murderers, looting and pillaging wherever they went. It is not surprising that by the eleventh century there was a reaction against these "wandering monks" or *gyrovagues* as they were called. Indeed, the very first chapter of the *Rule of St. Benedict* notes that of the four kinds of monks (Cenobites, Hermits, Sarabites who do not live by a Rule and therefore, "lie to God"), the most distasteful are the "Girovagi" about whom "it is better to say nothing."[78]

77. Merton, *Other Side of the Mountain*, 323.
78. Benedict, *Rule*, 13–15.

Section IV

This section explores the lure of the Crusades and provides an overview of the pilgrimages to Jerusalem and the Crusades to the East, noting that they "introduced a note of fatal ambiguity into the concept of pilgrimage and penance."[79] What was meant to be an act of great unification evolved into organized martial expeditions to attain and conquer by arms and politics the "holy place," the "promised land," the "place of resurrection." Sadly, Christian life devolved into a struggle with so-called "pagan" adversaries, and the Christian pilgrimage, once thought to be a "remedy for sins of violence," became a "consecration of violence."[80]

Section V

Merton's final section—perhaps surprisingly—focuses on the West as a "land of promise, " marking Columbus' voyage, as well as those of the Spanish *conquistadores*. The motive for his long distance travel echoes Brendan's quest for the "Lost Island" and the refuge sought from the attacks of the Norsemen. To be sure, this is a unique perspective. Merton views all the explorers, Puritans, missionaries, and colonizers of any stripe as significantly influenced by the mythical paradise aspect of America. They came to "begin again," yet fell into the lure and enjoyment of the riches found here. The land of new beginnings for self and society became a battleground against the wilderness and the infidel. This is a grim analysis of the settling of the Americas.[81] Despite this bleak picture, Merton's essay concludes with a reaffirmation of his initial premise: the necessity of pilgrimage "because it is an inescapable part of man's [*sic*] structure and program. The problem," Merton astutely notes, "is for his pilgrimage to make sense—it must represent a complete integration of his inner and outer life, of his relation to himself and to other men."[82] Here again, Merton reinforces his belief in the unity of matter and spirit, so ordained by the Creator. His final sentences are instructive and challenging:

79. Merton, "From Pilgrimage to Crusade," 200.

80. Ibid.

81. See *Conjectures of a Guilty Bystander*, 33–39 in which Merton discusses the false myth of America as an earthly paradise.

82. Ibid., 203.

If we instinctively seek a paradisiacal and special place on earth, it is because we know in our inmost hearts that the earth was given us in order that we might find meaning, order, truth, and salvation in it. The world is not only a vale of tears. There is joy in it some-where. Joy is to be sought, for the glory of God . . . Our task now is to learn that if we can voyage to the ends of the earth and there find *ourselves* in the aborigine who most differs from ourselves, we will have made a fruitful pilgrimage . . . Mere sitting at home and meditating on the divine presence is not enough for our time. We have to come to the end of a long journey and see that the stranger we meet there is no other than ourselves—which is the same as saying that we find Christ in him . . . We are all pieces of the paradise isle, and we can find our Brendan's island only when we all realize ourselves together as the paradise which is Christ and His Bride, God, man, and Church.[83]

From Brendan to pilgrimage to Crusade: Merton once again demonstrates how his wide-ranging interests, coupled with scholarly ability to dig deep into a topic, make him a monk to be listened to and emulated. Borrowing from the Greek poet Archilochus, Ron Dart has playfully dubbed Merton both fox and hedgehog, one who excels in thinking both broadly and deeply.[84] Not only was Merton deeply interested in the monastic practices of the Celts and reading every book on the topic he could get his hands on, but he was also captivated by their cultural practices, their art and their literature. He was indeed both fox and hedgehog.

83. Ibid., 203–4.
84. Dart, "Thomas Merton," 14.

4

The Trinity in Nature and the Arts

All historical studies of the early Celts who lived throughout Europe before gravitating to Gaul, Britain, and Ireland highlight their devotion to nature and a world inhabited by spirits. To the ancient Greeks, the Celts were their "mysterious neighbors" who preferred living in natural environments rather than urban settings, choosing wild or cultivated landscape over highly organized societies. These pre-Christian Celts (similar to the Greek Fathers of the church) made no distinction between the sacred and the profane, believing that mountains, forests, and springs—indeed, all creation—were manifestations of the Divine. As Canadian theologian David B. Perrin notes: "in Christian Celtic spirituality, God, or perhaps more accurately, the Divine Presence, was recognized intensely in the workings of nature and was easily discerned in the landscapes of Ireland, Scotland, and England. For the Celts there was a sacredness to everyday place."[1] Spirits of the water were givers of life; spirits of the skies controlled patterns of wind, rain, and thunder; spirits of the trees—especially the oak, ash, and yew—created ceremonial meeting places. The Celts had special fondness for high places such as hills and mountains, and the lure of this tradition of "kings and saints and scholars and poets whose names still cling about the places that they knew" created legends of these holy places. Known as *dindshenchas*, these legends evolved into a body of literature, a kind of "Dictionary of National Topography."[2] Similar to Native American tradition, animals such as birds, wolves, snakes, and deer were seen as messengers of the spirits in the Otherworld that existed side by side with this concrete reality. The Welsh, in particular, believed that hunting the stag would lead the

1. Perrin, *Studying Christian Spirituality*, 59. See also Davies, *Celtic Spirituality*, 10–12.

2. Flower, *Irish Tradition*, 1.

hunter to the Otherworld. More widely known and celebrated in stories of several cultures is the beaver ("broad-tailed otter" in Gaelic), revered not only for its meat and oil, but also for its wood-working ability, a skill that became a model or totem for Celtic artisans. Gerald of Wales, in his delightful twelfth-century chronicle, *Journey through Wales*, recounts the description and activities of the beaver, who would even castrate itself to give the hunter his prize and thus escape with its life.[3]

The Celtic way of seeing—their great gift of imagination—touched every part of their lives. The seasonal rhythms of nature, for example, determined the Celtic calendar, each season heralded with festivals, music, and dancing. The Celtic New Year began on the first of November after the harvest, and the first of February signaled the beginning of spring and time for planting. Once Christianity took root among the Celts, it was an "easy sell" to change Druid feast days to celebration of Christian saints. November first became All Saints Day and February first, originally dedicated to Brigid, the Celtic goddess of fire and the hearth, became the feast day of fifth-century Abbess and Saint, Brigid of Kildare.

What is truly remarkable is that the essential aspect of the ancient Celts and then the Christian Celts—a way of seeing the goodness in all creation and acknowledging the Word as both creator and redeemer—permeated their worldview. They, as well as Thomas Merton in the 1960s, would have had no scientific data to underscore their beliefs. They could not have known, for example, about the exploding primeval fireball responsible for the ongoing creation of our universe, nor be able to count the number of light years to Alpha Centauri, our nearest star, yet they had a sense that God, humanity, and earth were a trinity of sacred interaction. Their firm adherence to the doctrine of the Trinity and the outpouring of the Father through the Incarnation of Jesus in the Holy Spirit enabled them to honor the simultaneous transcendence and immanence of the Divine and to see everything as holy.

Celts thought of the material world—landscape, for example—as not dead but alive, respiring with divine breath, wild with a fierce Presence. The late John O'Donohue was fond of calling attention to the Atlantic Ocean washing up against the rocky overhang and breathing up sounds—a veritable conversation between water and stone.[4] The pulse of the elements

---

3. Gerald of Wales, *Journey through Wales*, 174–77. This story of the beaver appears also in a sixth-century version of Aesop's fables.

4. O'Donohue, "A Celtic Pilgrimage."

was a clear sign to the Celts of the Divine Presence dwelling among them. Even silent stone walls, rough and ill-shaped as they were, proclaimed what O'Donohue calls "the integration of the awkward." Thomas Merton in the 1950s captured something of this insight in his poem "In Silence":

> Be still.
> Listen to the stones of the wall.
> Be silent, they try
> To speak your
> Name.
> Listen
> To the living walls.

He concludes the poem with a penetrating question: how can you not recognize that

> All their silence
> Is on fire?[5]

For the Celtic imagination, harmony of the elements and the Otherworld was a primal and primary experience. There was no split between matter and spirit. They understood that matter and spirit interpenetrate one another. Indeed, they anticipated Teilhard de Chardin's insight that "At the heart of matter is the heart of God."[6] These Celts were quick to celebrate their kinship with humans and non-humans and delighted in telling stories of this connectedness, particularly connectedness with animals who were often seen as messengers from the Otherworld.

Celtic scholar Esther de Waal is also fond of relating tales—legends and myths that might contain some factual elements—to demonstrate this kinship in which "we *receive* from earth's creatures . . . not from above."[7] In one such story, St. Kevin was at his monastery at Glendalough in Ireland praying in a trance-like state with cupped hands when a blackbird arrived to lay eggs in his nest-like palms. Legend claims that Kevin remained in this position until the chicks hatched in his tender hands. Then there is the example of St. Cuthbert from Lindisfarne in Scotland praying all night in the icy waters of the North Sea, after which small sea otters lay down beside him, rubbing against his ankles to warm them.[8] Many of the monks had

5. Merton, *Collected Poems*, 280–81.
6. Quoted by Newell, *Christ of the Celts*, 96.
7. De Waal, "Introduction to Celtic Spirituality."
8. Ibid. See also Waddell, *Beasts and Saints*, 59–61.

animal friends—a way of satisfying their desire for community. We are told that Marbán had a pet pig; Moling a fly, wren, and cat; and Mochua had a cock to wake him for Vigils, a mouse to lick his ear if he fell asleep at prayer, and a fly to keep his place in the psalter.[9]

Such vignettes make us instantly think of St. Francis of Assisi and create a sense of awe that the Celts anticipated his sacramental view of nature by several centuries. Merton was fond of telling his novices that the early Celtic monks were very Franciscan. In summer, the cenobites—with permission of their abbot—could "hop in a boat and find an island for the summer," eat fish and seagull eggs, and then return to their monastery.[10] More recently, Daniel Horan OFM has documented how Merton, early on, possessed a Franciscan heart. He was significantly influenced by the Franciscan intellectual tradition of Bonaventure who saw the *vestigia* [footprints] of God in all of nature; and he was influenced as well as by the writings of the Celtic theologian Duns Scotus who highlighted God's delight in creating the *haecceitas* [this-ness] of each individual creature. One of Merton's favorite saints, Angela of Foligno, is credited with declaring that the "world is pregnant with God."[11] This theological tradition of intimacy between nature and the Divine informed Merton's contemplation, yet he was equally influenced by his hands-on experience and love of the Olean hills and the Kentucky knobs, his delight in the migrating warblers, and his acknowledgement that we are a part of nature. Multiple references to nature in Merton's journals reveal recognition of Francis's influence—a kinship model that social ethicist Keith Douglas Warner asserts celebrates relationship, promotes courtesy, reflects a commitment to practice penance, and motivates us to be environmental peacemakers.[12]

Such a view of the holiness and power of nature is reflected in two early Merton poems, "Duns Scotus" and "Hymn for the Feast of Duns Scotus."[13] In the first, a celebration of the Blessed Virgin Mary, Merton acknowledges through military imagery, reminiscent of Anglo-Saxon keenings or the poetry of Gerard Manley Hopkins, the lances, blades, and banners that accompany the "music of Our Lady's army!" Yet because we are weak and suspicious, we have no way to comprehend the lofty theology of Scotus.

---

9. Flower, *Irish Tradition*, 60.

10. Merton, Tape #175.3 (March 10, 1968).

11. Horan, *Franciscan Heart*, 103, 132, 169.

12. Ibid., 149–50 quoting Warner, *Franciscan Theology of Environment*, 370.

13. Merton, *Collected Poems*, 164–65, 198–99.

We can only pledge our allegiance to the Virgin and admire Scotus as he emerges and "shakes his golden locks / And sings like the African sun."

In the second poem, Merton visits the unique landscape of this world—the *haecceitas* of the colored hills, woods, grasses, waters—and through the writings of Scotus is invited into a deeper understanding of the Trinity who is not only One, but also Love. The poem explores Merton's reaction to Scotus's claim of "Three Lovers, loving One another," a theological puzzle that enflames and energizes Merton so that at the Beloved's call, he is awakened anew. Being both dead and alive, Merton admits his heart is "held fast in that Three-Personed Love." He even experiences a moment of ecstasy in the Beloved's grasp so that the "whole universe swells with Thy wide-open speed / Father, the world bursts, breaks, huge Spirit, with Thy might" and "God sings victory, sings victory."

In addition to a pronounced kinship with all creation and celebration of the intersection of the Divine, the human, and the earth, the Celts had a deep understanding of the sacredness of place. Even though all landscape is holy, certain locations were and are still celebrated as particularly hallowed. As esteemed American essayist Scott Russell Sanders reminds us, certain natural formations "concentrate our experience of the land. We cannot hold the entire earth or even a forest or river in our minds at once; we need smaller places to apprehend and visit . . . to seek the power that made us."[14] Often referred to as "thin places,"[15] the Celts believe that in certain land formations the Divine Presence is even more perceptible and the Otherworld is palpably interlaced with this one. Twentieth-century Scottish Presbyterian minister George MacLeod (credited with describing the Holy Spirit as a "wild goose") notes that the air of the eternal is always "seeping through the physical."[16] More recently, National Public Radio correspondent Eric Weiner observed that in these "'thin places' heaven and earth collapse; in their spiritual power, we are transformed, unmasked so that we become our essential selves."[17]

There is an ancient Celtic saying that heaven and earth are three feet apart. Some believe that in the thin places, the distance is even smaller. Sacred places are not limited to officially sacred locations like churches or

---

14. Sanders, "Telling the Holy," 154–69.

15. De Waal, "A Fresh Look," 31. De Waal identifies Evelyn Underhill as the originator of this phrase in her 1937 lecture on "Education and the Spirit of Worship."

16. Quoted by Newell, *Listening for the Heartbeat of God*, 86.

17. Weiner, "Where Heaven and Earth."

basilicas; for the Celts, they were most often wild landscapes such as groves of trees, stone walls, mountains, or springs of water revered for the immediacy and healing presence of the Divine. Windswept islands such as Iona, the rocky peaks of Croagh Patrick, the cliffs of St. David, and the stretch of the Wye valley also give us a glimpse of the expansive power of the Divine. I am reminded of William Wordsworth, in the late 1790s, overlooking the ruins of Tintern Abbey in the Wye Valley of Wales and sensing what he calls a "presence" whose dwelling is everywhere in nature and in the human imagination:

> . . . And I have felt
> A presence that disturbs me with the joy
> Of elevated thoughts; a sense sublime
> Of something far more deeply interfused,
> Whose dwelling is the light of setting suns;
> And the round ocean and the living air,
> And the blue sky, and in the mind of man:
> A motion and a spirit, that impels
> All thinking things, all objects of all thought,
> And rolls through all things.[18]

Once we experience a sacred place, once we are more attuned to an expansive way of seeing that encourages us to recognize and be in awe of all creatures and one other, we begin to understand more deeply the import of an ancient Celtic blessing:

> Deep peace of the running wave to you
> Deep peace of the flowing air to you
> Deep peace of the quiet earth to you
> Deep peace of the shining stars to you
> Deep peace of the Son of Peace to you.[19]

Water, too, was especially important for the Celts. Springs, such as the Pool of Segais, and wells, such as Coventina's Well and the many Ladywells scattered throughout the Isles, were particularly revered as the primal source of everything on earth. In fact, the Celts believed that the earth floated on water which is the touchstone of Wisdom and the gateway to the mysterious inner life of the earth. Hence, the water cycle itself possesses its own enigmatic sacredness by bubbling up from springs, evaporating into air, and falling again to increase the fecundity of the earth. No wonder it

18. Wordsworth, "Lines Composed," 93–102.

19. Carmichael, *Carmina Gadelica*.

was considered *living* water, reminiscent of both baptism and consecration to Christ.

Thomas Merton had a similar fascination with water. His mother Ruth Jenkins Merton recorded in the baby book she was keeping for the New Zealand relatives that in Prades, France, baby Tom would stand up in his pram whenever they were approaching the bridge over the River Têt to see what he could already hear bubbling, gurgling, and tripping over the stones in the river bed.[20] In later years, Merton's poetic, yet challenging, essay "Rain and the Rhinoceros" celebrates the rain's "gratuity." Merton in his woods listens to it "because it reminds me again and again that the whole world runs by rhythms I have not yet learned to recognize, rhythms that are not those of the engineer." The wisdom of water in the form of rain, for Merton, is a "whole world of meaning, of secrecy, of silence, of rumor . . . all that speech pouring down, selling nothing, judging nobody, drenching the thick mulch of dead leaves, soaking the trees, filling the gullies and crannies of the wood with water."[21]

Supporting this incarnational view of nature is the Celtic belief in the Holy Trinity, derived originally from explanations by the Cappadocian Fathers in the East and embedded in Celtic daily practice. Because the heart of God—Father, Son, Spirit—is essentially a community of Persons, a dance of overflowing Love, we who are made in God's image find our fulfillment in relationship. The Celts were not fixated on three separate and individual Persons of God: the Father *and* the Son *and* the Holy Spirit. Rather, as Merton explained to his novices in a Conference May 24, 1964, the Celts understood the importance, even necessity, of *relationship* among the Persons. "They honored the Father *through* the Son *in* the Holy Ghost." Because the Son is consubstantial with the Father, we humans are divinized; because the Spirit dwells in me, directing me to the Father, we can say with St. Paul "When we cry 'Abba! Father!' it is that very Spirit bearing witness with our spirit that we are children of God."[22] This Eastern Orthodox understanding of the mystery of Trinity as *one nature* was as important for Merton as it was for the early Celts. The Trinity is simultaneously creating, saving, and sanctifying all of creation. Myriad hymns, prayers, poems, household

---

20. Merton, *Tom's Book*, n.p.
21. Merton, "Rain and the Rhinoceros," 9–10.
22. Rom 8:15–16, NRSV.

chants, and incantations testify to this belief, many of which have been collected by Alexander Carmichael in *Carmina Gadelica*.[23]

Acknowledgement of the holy and of the Trinity guided the *horarium* from dawn to dusk not only of fourth, fifth and sixth-century monks, but also of ordinary people who worked the land or managed a household. Psalms and sacramental rituals were adapted to household prayers as well as to prayers for sowing and reaping that reflected both the unity and orthodoxy of Celtic Christianity and the diversity of its expression. "Rhythms of three" were woven into common Celtic speech. Esther de Waal offers as poignant evidence of the pervasiveness of Trinitarian consciousness this simple and ancient chant:

> Three folds of cloth, yet only one napkin is there,
> Three joints in the finger, still only one finger fair
> Three leaves of the shamrock, yet no more than one shamrock to wear,
> Frost, snow-flakes, and ice, all in water their origin share
> Three Persons in God, to one God alone we make prayer.[24]

Rhymes and jingles based on triads of ideas are, for the common folk, a reminder of being steeped in Trinitarian love. At the birth of a child, for example, and prior to its clerical baptism, the mother or midwife pours three drops of water on its forehead in honor of the Trinity.[25] At the start of day, a woman, rising before her household, splashes her face with water, three times in honor of the Trinity. She makes her bed in the name of the Father, Son, and Holy Ghost and stirs the fire to life in the hearth, celebrating the new flame with a prayer of renewal. Calling on the angelic presences to fill her cottage with the Holy Son of God, she prays that a similar flame of love for the neighbor, the friend, the foe, "my kindred all," will be kindled in her heart. But she also pleads—in unique Celtic tradition—that this flame of love will extend to all creation, even to "the lowliest thing that liveth."[26] Her day ends with a banking of the fire ("smooring"), a ritual of laying down the peat in the name of the Trinity, saints and angels. This ritual was always performed carefully, symbolically, with loving care, the first "in the

---

23. Carmichael, *Carmina Gadelica*.

24. De Waal, *Celtic Way of Prayer*, 39–40 quoting from Eleanor Hall, *The Poem Book of the Gael*, 237.

25. De Waal, *Celtic Way of Prayer*, 28.

26. Ibid., 30–31.

name of the God of life, the second the God of peace, the third the God of grace," intoning a prayer "To save, To shield, To surround" her household.[27]

Notice that this prayer recognizes the unity of all that is. With low humming, crooning, and gestures such as lifting the peat three times, the woman of the house consecrates her day. Throughout the day, whether milking, churning butter ("Come ye rich lumps, come"), grinding corn, making cloth, or preparing a meal, the Trinity is invoked. De Waal notes that "quite apart from the fact that saying and doing something rhythmi-cally three times over fitted in so well with much of their daily work . . . [b]oth the action and the instrument were committed to God for his protec-tion and blessing."[28] Men, too, walking toward the fields, the sea, or the flocks, used the journey to and fro as a time to "walk with God and for God to walk with them."[29] This cross-fertilization of pre-Christian and Chris-tian practices, due largely to the pervasive influence of monasticism on the lives of ordinary people, says de Waal, preserved the "ancient oral lore" and raised the use of the vernacular to a "medium of Christian literature."[30]

Indeed, language itself, for the Celt, was grounded in the senses. Children were encouraged to "play the five-string harp," that is, to learn how to experience the world through their five senses. The world, for these ancient people, was not linear, but cyclical with recurring feasts and fes-tivities; hence, the imagination—and life itself—was always a doorway to the Holy. Through complex patterns and repeated motifs that connect idea and emotion, these Celts basked in an understanding of God and Christian discipleship as a "holy worldliness."[31] To this Celtic belief in the holiness of all creation, Allchin aptly applies the words of Teilhard de Chardin, "it seems appropriate . . . to speak of 'the Mass on the World.'"[32]

The Celtic way of *seeing*, that is both incarnational and a celebration of the Trinity, is so deeply embedded in the Celtic imagination that it over-flows into the visual arts, especially metal design, manuscript illumination, and stone work. The *triquetra* or three-cornered interlocking shapes, for example, have been found on rune stones in Northern Europe and the

---

27. Ibid., 47–48.

28. De Waal, *Every Earthly Blessing*, 4–8.

29. Ibid., 9.

30. De Waal, *Celtic Way of Prayer*, 35.

31. The phrase is attributed to Dietrich Bonhoeffer describing the twofold challenge of understanding God and radical Christian discipleship.

32. Allchin, *God's Presence*, xii.

British Isles. Because it predates Christianity, it is thought to have been a symbol of the Goddess (maid, mother, crone) that is often depicted as a three-fold collection of fishes (*vesica pisces*). Early on, it became a symbol of belief in the Father, Son, and Holy Spirit, but also represented natural forces of earth, air, and water; similarly, the *triquetra* was used as a reminder of life, death, and rebirth. Irish monks are thought to have added a circle behind the triangular shape to represent the eternity of God's love and/or the circle of life. Variations of this tri-foil are found on early creations of jewelry, swords, and plaques.

Celtic design in spirals and whirls, often called "plaiting" (related to our linguistic term for braiding hair), gradually evolved into more and more intricate geometric patterns. This pre-Christian art is thought to have traveled the same route as monasticism—from Egypt and North Africa to Italy, to southern Gaul, to Ireland—and was embraced by both Celtic monks and secular artists. Merton was fond of pointing out to his novices that the curved lines of Celtic art reveal the culture as "harmonious, organic" and "full of life."[33] Imaginative and often mis-proportioned plants, animals, and humans—again demonstrating the integration of the sacred and the secular—were incorporated into repetitive patterns on the cover or on carpet pages of illuminated manuscripts, most notably the Book of Kells.[34] Surviving also are the eighth-century Book of Chad, referred to as the Lichfield Gospels, which have the earliest examples of written Welsh in the margins,[35] the Book of Durrow, the Gospels of Lindisfarne, the tenth-century Book of Deer (Scotland), and the St. Gall Gospel. Dom Louis Gougaud, one of Merton's key sources for information on Celtic Christianity, offers an uncharacteristically effusive judgment that the "interlacement" of design, especially in the Book of Kells, created "labyrinths of ribbons and straps endlessly unrolled, crossing and recrossing one another in an extremely complicated and varied entanglement of lines without ever offending our eyes by a suggestion of disorder or confusion."[36] Judging from subtle differences in the penmanship of the scribe using a script called "insular majuscule"—developed by Irish monks as early as the seventh century and often attributed

---

33. Merton, Tape #124.2 (September 16, 1964).

34. Carpet pages are the first and final leaves of an illuminated manuscript, usually decorated with repeating geometric designs. Modern use can be found in daily prayer books such as Stommes, *Give Us This Day*.

35. Richardson, *Celtic Calligraphy*, 9.

36. Gougaud, *Christianity in Celtic Lands*, 377.

to St. Columba—expert calligrapher Kerry Richardson maintains that at least three scribes were engaged in creating the Book of Kells.[37] Usually in a book of the Gospels, each of the four Evangelists is celebrated on a carpet page that includes a totem: a Man for Matthew, a Lion for Mark, an Ox for Luke, and an Eagle for John. Such designs in the manuscripts, Merton remarked to his novices, were to underscore the close relationship of the Divine Office and contemplation. The designs and open space appealed to the visual imagination and encouraged meditation on a word. In somewhat the same way, Merton notes, Gregorian chant—which apparently the Irish did not use[38]—employs a decorative *neum* or *jubilus* over a particular Latin word so that, in the singing of it, one can savor the many levels of meaning. Merton's point about illuminated manuscripts is that the Irish spent time on a word, time to "squeeze it, eat it," linger over it, and that we need to read these texts with new contemplative eyes.[39] Esther de Waal argues that the point of the Lindisfarne Gospels, "finished about thirty years after Whitby, was to portray Cuthbert as 'the great Reconciler'" because the illustrations brought together "many traditions, Irish, English, Roman, and Coptic, blending them into one glorious and harmonious whole." Modern calligraphers regard these Gospels as "a visual statement of the unification of the various streams of Christian orthodoxy lived by the church in Northumbria at that time, at once both distinctly local and universal."[40]

Related to plait work, and often integrated into the design of a carpet page, are Celtic knots made of interlacing lines, repeating figures-of-eight, waves or semi-circles, whose meaning defies any modern attempt to assign symbolism to them. The basic explanation of knot work, which can be traced back to third-century Roman floor mosaics,[41] is that it epitomizes the timeless nature of the human spirit, the interlacing of the spiritual and the physical, birth and rebirth. The closed path of the knot denotes both eternity and the ever-present love of God. It is not surprising, then, as J. Philip Newell notes, that fourteenth-century anchoress Julian of Norwich used the image of the Celtic knot to "portray the strands of time and eternity intertwined, of the human and the creaturely inseparable interrelated,

---

37. Richardson, *Celtic Calligraphy*, 8, 20.

38. Gougaud, *Christianity in Celtic Lands*, 377–78.

39. Merton, Tape #125.1 (September 12, 1964).

40. De Waal, "A Fresh Look," 40.

41. Richardson, *Celtic Calligraphy*, 32.

of the one and the many forever married. Christ's soul and our soul are like an everlasting knot."[42]

The earliest surviving example of true Celtic knot work dates back to the seventh century and is preserved in the library of Durham Cathedral.[43] In one of his conferences, Thomas Merton encouraged his novices to cover their Breviary with plain paper and then "begin drawing abstract designs on it . . . seeing what might evolve from their imagination and the human need to create something beautiful."[44] (It strikes me that there may be a resonance with these early Celtic designs in the contemporary popularity of zentangles, meditatively drawn with pen and ink.) Merton himself was enchanted by Celtic artisan skill. In a September 24, 1964 letter to Hans Urs Von Balthasar, Merton comments that he is immersing himself in Celtic monasticism: "it is becoming a real avocation with me . . . I can think of nowhere in the West where monastic culture was so drenched in brilliant color and form, with such dazzled love of God's beauty."[45]

Many Celtic artisans had a particular devotion to working in stone because of its permanence and availability. Their carved stone crosses, which reflect the heart of their spirituality, evolved over time into elaborate "high crosses." Because Christ is viewed as coming from the heart of God and revealing to us what is at the heart of God's being, these high crosses represent both the love of Christ and creation.[46] Moreover, since the pattern of worship from the fourth to the seventh centuries was to gather around the crosses framed by earth, sea, and sky, the Celts demonstrated their belief that "creation itself [is] the Sanctuary of God."[47] The most beautiful, according to many, is Muiredach's High Cross found in the ruins of Monasterboice in County Louth.[48] Merton lectured several times to the novices about the art and theological import of this early Christian expression of faith, paying homage to the influence of the Desert Fathers, especially St. Anthony of Egypt and St. Paul the Hermit who are often depicted on them.[49] Merton adds a playful note in a September 5, 1964 journal entry: "Today—in con-

42. Newell, *Christ of the Celts*, 69.

43. Richardson, *Celtic Calligraphy*, 33.

44. Merton Tape #124.2 (September 5, 1964).

45. Merton, *School of Charity*, 241.

46. Newell, *Christ of the Celts*, 52.

47. Ibid., 110.

48. Richardson, *Celtic Calligraphy*, 33.

49. Merton, Tape # 124.2 (September 5, 1964).

ference—drawing primitive Celtic crosses on the blackboard. They seemed to enjoy it."[50] A few months earlier in *Working Notebook #14* dated June 1964, Merton drew on the flyleaf three high crosses with a crude half-circle under each of them. It was only after steeping myself in his notes on Celtic culture and listening to his conferences to the novices that I realized these half-circles with pointed ends were intended to represent anchors—another symbol of faith for these Celts who lived by the sea and often risked the treachery of its waters.

In some early depictions of the cross or "tree of life," a great round circle occurs at the juncture of the horizontal arms, possibly signifying both creation and redemption. There is some debate about the meaning of this circle. In a February 2014 videotaped lecture at St. Paul's Cathedral, London, Esther de Waal offered her insight based on her extensive research into Celtic spirituality.[51] Perhaps, she said, the circle symbolizes the Druid sun, the Roman victory laurel, the cosmos, or the halo of Christ. In any event, the circle and the cross—that is, the "hands of God"—hold in tension *Christus Victor*, a Christ who speaks to us, who has set us free, who holds death and life together. In an earlier publication de Waal suggests that the high crosses, often with widely recognized Biblical figures carved into the long vertical base, functioned as a kind of "visual *lectio divina*,"—a visual aid for catechesis of the illiterate and a reminder to all the faithful of important episodes of Christian salvation history.[52] As for the intricate geometric designs on the cross-arms, these mandala-like spirals may have been intended to encourage contemplation. The high cross of Saint Martin on Iona, for example, devotes one side to scripture imagery and the other side to creation imagery. J. Philip Newell reminds us: "Both belong to the cross design. Both are read in Christ."[53] Whatever their intent, maintains de Waal, because of the centrality of Christ to the Celtic experience, this particular religious expression should not be thought of as creation-centered spirituality, but rather as *creation-filled* spirituality. This distinction is an important one, she maintains, because of the unique Celtic gift of imagination that embraces a "glorious enjoyment of the whole created universe."[54] Merton, writing about prayer in *Contemplation in a World of*

50. Merton, *Dancing in the Water*, 142.

51. De Waal, "An Introduction to Celtic Spirituality."

52. De Waal, *Celtic Way of Prayer*, 143.

53. Newell, *Christ of the Celts*, 52.

54. De Waal, *Celtic Way of Prayer*, 141.

Action, understood clearly the power of imagination and its function to discover and deepen faith:

> Imagination has the creative task of making symbols, joining things together in such a way that they throw new light on each other and on everything around them. The imagination is a discovering faculty, a faculty for seeing relationships, for seeing meanings that are special and even quite new. The imagination is something which enables us to discover unique present meaning in a given moment of our life. Without imagination the contemplative life can be extremely dull and fruitless.[55]

While not specifically writing about the Celtic tradition, Merton nevertheless captures the essence of the Celtic way of seeing and expressing this worldview in its art—an ability for symbol-making and intuiting relationships, a penchant for discovering the "everywhere" God who is simultaneously immanent and transcendent—and celebrating that God not only in formal monastic rituals, but also in common everyday living. Such a gift is not to be regarded naively, but rather extolled, emulated, shared, and integrated into one's spirituality.

Integration is precisely what Thomas Merton desired for his novices. During the spring and summer of 1964, after he had presented conferences on Irish and Syrian monasticism, the Eastern understanding of the Trinity, and prayer advice from the Desert Fathers, Merton made two presentations on Art and Beauty in which he looked at the big picture of what is necessary for human fulfillment.[56] "There is beauty we contribute to and beauty we respond to." Merton was very strong in his insistence that "Life without beauty can't be Christian life . . . grace implies beauty and this applies to liturgy as well. Worship has to be meaningful, beautiful."[57] His conference went on to explain how a beautiful face is only a sign of beauty. Beauty is the fullness of "being itself—the more being, the more beauty." A tree, for example, is beautiful insofar as it is *this* tree—with all its particularities, its *haecceitas* or this-ness, as Gerard Manley Hopkins would phrase it. Offering a brief philosophical explanation of the distinction between substance

55. Merton, *Contemplation in a World of Action*, 345.

56. Merton, Tape # 122.4 (August 12, 1964) and Tape # 123.3 (August 22, 1964). During this time, Merton was also working on notes for an article on art and morality for the *New Catholic Encyclopedia* 1 (864–67).

57. Merton, Tape 122.4. In the early 1960s Merton commissioned several pieces of art for the novitiate chapel to be created by his artist friend Victor Hammer. See Scutchfield and Holbrook, *Letters of Thomas Merton*, 85, 89.

("is-ness") and accident (properties of a being), Merton makes the point that beauty is not the perfection of an essence or something like "icing on the cake." Rather, beauty is something individual, and this is where Art comes in. Each tree, each creature is a work of God's Art, and all humans are invited to share in God's creative artistry by making beautiful things— even, Merton says, a thing as simple as a carefully made bed.

Merton's words certainly echo chapter 3 of *Seeds of Contemplation* (1949) and chapter 5 of *New Seeds of Contemplation* (1962), in which he celebrates the *haecceitas*, the this-ness or inscape of particular forms whose "inscape is their sanctity." Echoing Gerard Manley Hopkins's notion of in-scape, Merton writes: "Each particular being in its individuality, its concrete nature and entity, with all its own characteristics and its private qualities and its own inviolable identity gives glory to God by being precisely what He wants it to be here and now, in the circumstances ordained for it by His Love and His infinite Art." [58] Merton illustrates his point with the "clumsy beauty of this particular colt," the "pale flowers of the dogwood outside this window," this leaf with "its own texture . . . and pattern of veins," the "lakes hidden among the hills," the sea, and the "great, gashed, half-naked mountain"—all are God's saints because of "the imprint of His wisdom and His reality in them."[59]

Of course, the challenge comes when we speak of humanity. We have the freedom "to be real or to be unreal," and here Merton adds a new, lengthy paragraph to *New Seeds* that is not in the original 1949 edition—an insight that Merton surely had come to grasp through his own prayer and solitude. "Our vocation is not simply to *be*, but to work together with God in the creation of our own life, our own identity, our own destiny." That identity, as Merton articulates it, can only be discovered in the gift of con-templation.[60] Merton's counsel echoes the wisdom of Irish theologian John Scotus Eriugena that nature offers us the gift of "being," but grace—prayer, contemplation— offers us the gift of "well-being."[61]

These late summer seminars for the novices set the stage for Septem-ber conferences focused on early Celtic and monastic art that so intrigued Merton, primarily the Celts' "astonishing power of imagination."[62] Merton

---

58. Merton, *New Seeds of Contemplation*, 30.

59. Ibid., 30–31.

60. Ibid., 32–33.

61. Newell, *Christ of the Celts*, 9.

62. Jackson, *Celtic Miscellany*, 12.

wanted the novices to delight—as he did—in the intricacies of their designs on carpet pages, the elongation of humans and animals within illuminated letters on manuscripts, and the deep aesthetic and theological meaning of the high crosses found throughout the Celtic lands. As Newell notes so well, "Celtic spirituality is more poetic than doctrinal." [63] This is not to diminish in any way its theological significance. By contemplating the work of the artist, Merton remarked, we come to know something of the inner life of the artist. Thus by contemplating nature, "we come to know the mind of God through his creatures . . . God is all the time talking, speaking in works of art." Certainly, admits Merton, the words of the Bible are God's revelation, but the "Word is God's most limited form of communication." God is "profuse in communicating via creation" which is his "cosmic art." Indeed, "God's art in me allows me to participate in cosmic art" just as a little child imitates his father making things in the basement or garage. When we are aware of our surroundings, real beauty, real art gives more than sensual pleasure; it gives a higher spiritual pleasure and is, thus, a "step toward the vision of God."[64] Although Merton does not quote Bernard of Clairvaux in these conferences, he surely echoes St. Bernard's counsel: "You will find something more in woods than in books. Trees and stones will teach you that which you can never learn from masters."[65] It takes intelligence, not learning or education, comments Merton, to understand art. "If one's intelligence is whole, one can apprehend beauty on all levels, including beauty of God."[66]

Consequently, says Merton, one of our human roles is to work against ugliness ("a lack of due being") by restoring things to their fullness of being, that is, their beauty. Merton offers as examples of what he means activities such as the art of forestry, gardening, medicine, and harmony in the liturgy—ways in which humans are called to "make things" that offer more than mere sensual pleasure. If, as Merton wrote in his opening paragraph of his 1959 article, "Art and Worship," human beings are made in the image of God, then we have a vocation not only to function within the world, "but to transform it and to draw from it the hidden glory which has been placed in creation by its creator. Hence man [*sic*] cannot be complete if he is only a scientist and a technician: he must also be an artist and a contemplative"— roles that bring society into harmony. According to Merton's thinking, "art

63. Newell, *Christ of the Celts*, 84.

64. Merton, Tape #122.4 (August 12, 1964) and Tape #123.3 (August 22, 1964).

65. Bernard of Clairvaux, *The Letters of St. Bernard of Clairvaux*, Epistle 106.

66. Merton, Tape #123.3.

has a vitally important place not only in keeping man civilized but also in helping him to 'save his soul,' that is to say, to live as a Child of God who has knowledge, understanding and love of the things of his Father." [67]

In addition to Celtic knots and high crosses, Merton was vitally interested in Irish oral literature and the poems created by the educated hermits, many of whom were scribes often adding their own thoughts in the margins of the vellum they were working on. For monks, copying manuscripts was more than busy-work. It was part of a long legacy of Christian ministry. As Kuno Meyer has argued: "We would hardly have any record of early Anglo Saxon literature if the English had not in the first instance received Christianity from the Irish. It was the influence and example of these Irish missionaries who converted Northumberland that taught the Anglian monk to preserve and cultivate his national literature." [68] The next chapter will look more closely at Merton's interest in contemporary Welsh poetry and his fascination with Celtic hermit poetry—"the vernacular literature of ancient Ireland" that Kuno Meyer regards as "the most primitive and original among the literatures of Western Europe." [69]

67. Merton, "Art and Worship," 114–17.

68. Meyer, *Selections from Ancient Irish Poetry*, ix.

69. Ibid., vii.

5

Contemporary Welsh Poetry
and Early Irish Hermit Poetry

B eing trained in literature, Thomas Merton was naturally curious about other Celtic artistic expressions, namely poetry. In his reading and conversations with Donald Allchin, he began to understand Allchin's particular fondness for the Welsh language and culture—that would later coalesce in Allchin's book on the Celtic vision in ancient Wales.[1] The Welsh, whose pre-Christian sense of an "iron fate which determines all things" was succeeded by a "vision of human life in all its fragility as open to the eternity of God. This is not only an openness to an eternity beyond this world, it is an openness to an eternal life already made known and experienced now."[2] These Celts living in the southwestern part of Britain, fiercely clinging to their Welsh heritage, maintains Allchin, have a striking "sense that God's grace is present and at work now, evident in the diversity and richness of creation, and in the way in which apparent opposites belong together and are at one." One of the oldest theological poems, traceable to the tenth century, has marginalia written in Latin, Welsh, and Irish, supporting the belief that Welsh and Irish monks lived together in community. The existing fragment of "In Praise of the Trinity" reflects the metrical structure and overlapping, cyclical patterns of earlier sixth-century oral secular praise poetry. Because God was worshipped as creator, redeemer, and sanctifier, poetry was considered a "divine gift" but one that must be cultivated.[3]

Early Welsh poetry, as Allchin was discovering and no doubt sharing with Merton during his visits, had a "deliberately incarnational framework." In tune with their northern Irish cousins, they saw the world as a

1. Allchin, *God's Presence*, 5–7.

2. Ibid., 4.

3. Ibid., 8–10.

place of God's presence and ongoing creation, immersed in the mystery of dying and rising, and exemplifying both diversity and coherence.[4] The ninth-century theologian, John Scotus Eriugena (c. 810–877), a scholar living at a time when Ireland, Britain, and the continent were in frequent contact, taught that creation and redemption are not two, but one outpouring of a loving God: "That which is properly thought of as beyond all essence is also properly known in all essence and therefore every visible and invisible creature can be called a theophany, that is an appearance of the divine."[5] This balance of transcendence and immanence is consistent with the earlier seventh-century Greek theologian Maximus the Confessor who, among other theologians, "used the doctrine of the uncreated energies of God to underline the fact that God holds us all together with himself by reason of his active suffering with all . . . For the energies of God are not shut in on themselves but come out into the world and are active throughout creation."[6] Or as Donald Allchin phrases it: "God comes out of himself into his world both in creation and redemption."[7] This seemingly *avant garde* notion to Western ears resonates with Pope Francis's first General Audience in which he speaks of God stepping out of God's Self by creating the universe, and again stepping out into humanity in the Person of Jesus—adding that we also are called to imitate Jesus by stepping out of ourselves to serve one another.[8]

Contemporary Welsh Poets

In conjunction with his study of the early Celts in Wales, Donald Allchin was also reading modern Welsh poets, inheritors of the ancient Celtic tradition that "has lived in a certain isolation from the outside world and has jealously guarded its own inner coherence and integrity."[9] In the course of his correspondence with Merton between 1963 and 1968, Allchin was pleased to recommend three such authors: R. S. Thomas, the twentieth-century poet and Anglican country priest, David Jones, an innovative Catholic modern-

---

4. Ibid., 10–14.

5. Eriugena quoted by Allchin, *God's Presence*, 16.

6. Maximus quoted by Allchin, *God's Presence*, 22. See also Davies, *Celtic Spirituality*, 28.

7. Allchin, *God's Presence*, 22.

8. Francis I, "First General Audience."

9. Allchin, *God's Presence*, xiii.

ist painter and poet, and Ann Griffith, an eighteenth-century mystic and evangelical hymn-writer in Welsh, whose work has influenced several contemporary writers including R. S. Thomas and Rowan Williams.[10]

Imagine Merton's delight at finding three new poets to read, poets who were steeped in Welsh lore and culture! Merton deemed R. S. Thomas a "marvelous discovery"; he was "completely swept away" by David Jones; and he considered Ann Griffith, along with R. S. Thomas, a potential candidate for a quoted piece in *Monk's Pond*, Merton's little 1968 experimental magazine of prose and poetry.[11] These poets formed a valuable Celtic trinity of "study" for Merton during the last years of his life. Although we don't know exactly which poems Merton read, he might well have savored lines from R. S. Thomas' poem, "A Welsh Testament," finding them *simpatico* with his own impatience with noise around the monastery that, in a real sense, tainted the pristine quality of nature.

> . . . I saw them stare
> From their long cars, as I passed knee-deep
> In ewes and wethers. I saw them stand
> By the thorn hedges, watching me string
> The far flocks on a shrill whistle.
> And always there were their eyes; strong
> Pressure on me: You are Welsh, they said;
> Speak to us so; keep your fields free
> Of the smell of petrol, the loud roar
> Of hot tractors; we must have peace
> And quietness.[12]

As for David Jones, whose poetry T. S. Eliot considered a "work of genius" because of his finely shaped "landscape of language," Donald Allchin encouraged Merton to write to Jones, a semi-recluse struggling with depression. Allchin was in personal contact with Jones, including a four-hour chat with the aging poet who "lives in one large totally chaotic room in a small 'private hotel' . . . P.S. I am so glad that you take to D. Jones

---

10. Ibid., 85.

11. Merton, *Hidden Ground of Love*, 28–30. Four issues of *Monks' Pond* were published in 1968, but no work of either Griffith or Thomas was included. Originally the magazine was printed in runs of 150–200 copies on inexpensive paper, and its circulation confined to contributors. A *facsimile* illustrated copy of *Monk's Pond* was published by the University Press of Kentucky in July 1989.

12. Thomas, "A Welsh Testament."

so strongly. It has been one of the *great* discoveries for me this last year."[13] Jones's epic work, *In Parenthesis* (1937) details his experience of World War I and *The Anathemata* (1952) focuses on British history and mythology. These lengthy pieces have been touted as major contributions to Welsh poetry, primarily because of Jones's sacramental view of nature. As Welsh poet and literary critic Saunders Lewis has written of Jones's artistic output for an exhibition in 1954:

> The past is all a now, the eternal in the petal, the branches in the clay of a teapot and in the brittleness of glass. The earth herself in her alert pain dreams of the hand that has shaped her. No man nor place stands alone. The scapegoat of Israel is caught in the barbed wire of 1915 and the trees of the field walk in through the windows of your house. David Jones is an artist who affirms that the vision in the final canto of Dante's *Paradise* is an ever contemporary fact.[14]

No wonder both Allchin and Merton were swept away by this poetic giant.

In March of 1968, Allchin sent Merton some poems of Ann Griffith, translated by H. A. Hodges—primarily for his reading pleasure and perhaps for inclusion in Merton's *Monk's Pond*. (Allchin was at the time working on his own translations of the poems that he published eight years later in the Writers of Wales series.[15]) Allchin loved the "theological richness of Ann's spiritual vision" and her "Anglican wonder in the power of the Incarnation [that] fuses with an evangelical longing for eternity."[16] Allchin believed that although Griffith had little formal education, "Hers was a knowledge received through prayer and sacrament, through faith and obedience, in the silence of prayer and adoration."[17] Had she lived in another time, he speculated, she would probably have been a member of a monastic community.[18] Indeed, Allchin believed a poet has a dual role to fill: a "priestly role, speaking on behalf of his fellow human beings and on behalf of all creation."[19] As evidence of this belief and fondness for Griffith's poetry, Allchin, from time

---

13. Allchin, unpublished letter to Merton (February 5, 1968), Louisville, KY: Thomas Merton Center.

14. Quoted by Allchin, *God's Presence*, 137–38.

15. See Allchin, *Ann Griffiths*.

16. Allchin, *Songs To Her God*, vi.

17. Ibid., 4.

18. Ibid., 65.

19. Allchin, *God's Presence*, xii.

to time, sent Merton some of his own translations of Griffith's poetry[20] and in 1987 he published a study of her life and work entitled *Songs to Her God*.

Although we do not have documentation of what Allchin actually sent to Merton, these poignant lines from the fourth verse of Hymn #5 about the "Sea of wonders" and the "Sea where none can find a shore" would have resonated with Merton and his love for the Celtic practice of *peregrinatio*. Notice, too, how the hymn is grounded in the Trinity:

> Blessed hour of rest eternal,
> Home at last, all labours o'er;
> Sea of wonders never sounded,
> Sea where none can find a shore;
> Access free to dwell for ever
> Yonder with the One in Three;
> Deeps no foot of man can traverse—
> God and man in unity.

In the third verse of Hymn #6 about "The Way," the poet understands that even the bird's eye of the high-flying kite [falcon-like raptor] cannot discern what faith reveals:

> Eye of kite could ne'er discern it, [the Way]
> Though it shines with noontide blaze;
> None can tread it, none can see it,
> Save where faith its light displays;[21]

Merton was fond of discussing monastic spirituality in terms of "the Way." In a January 1963 conference to the novices, he talks about the nineteenth-century rediscovery by the Greek Metropolitan of Nicomedia of the *Didache*, the first or second-century teaching of the Apostles that outlines the Two Ways: one of life and one of death. For Merton, the ideal Way can be found in chapters 6 and 7 of Matthew's Gospel: "Do not be anxious" and "Enter by the narrow gate." The Synoptic Gospel writers, Merton remarks to the novices, offer the monk counsel on the "Way of Faith, not the Way of Doubt." Yet even more than these guidelines for conduct is the perspective offered in St. John's Gospel: "I am the Way." Finding Christ, says Merton, is going beyond the Way to respond to the invitation to "Abide in Me." Merton's challenge to these young monks is to "Start with the Synoptic sense,

---

20. Donald Allchin gave a series of lectures in Bangor in 1996, using some of Ann Griffith's poetry, later published in *God's Presence Makes the World*, 1997.

21. Griffith, *Hymns*.

then move to John and the contemplative way" because the essence of monastic life is "abiding in Christ, no floundering around. Sink into it and be content."[22] This kind of grounding in the monastic life, a grounding that is alert to the beauties of creation and the presence of God is what Merton saw revealed so explicitly in the early Celtic culture.

Early Irish Hermit Poetry

Merton's lyrics

Merton himself during these years was reading not only the Welsh poets that both he and Allchin found inspiring, but also early Irish hermit poetry. Their Celtic gift of imaginative vision is celebrated by Kuno Meyer in his introduction to *Ancient Irish Poetry*: "to seek out and watch and love Nature, in its tiniest phenomena as in its grandest, was given to no people so early and so fully as to the Celt."[23] Merton, who himself was a poet,[24] was captivated by early Irish poetry and was even trying his hand at his own lyrics on Celtic figures. One such attempt, "St Maedoc (Fragment of an Ikon)" appears in handwritten form in *Working Notebook #14* (June 1964) after several pages of notes about Celtic high crosses, the Rule of Tallaght, books on ancient Irish poetry, and an outline of the events of St. Brendan's sea journey. Merton's original poem celebrates an early sixth-century Irish or Welsh monk, founder of the monastery of Ferns and legendary miracle worker noted for his benevolence and hospitality. Also known as Mogue and Aidan, Maedoc was educated in Wales at St. David's monastery, taking with him a "carload of beer" to this notoriously abstemious monastery. He later returned to Ireland.[25]

Merton's poem refers to several of the miracles associated with the saint: the "floating stone" that ferried him as an infant across a lake when no boat was available, the transformation of the visage of "Aed Duv, son

---

22. Merton, Tape #41.4 (January 30, 1963).

23. Meyer, *Ancient Irish Poetry*, xii.

24. Merton wrote his M.A. thesis on "Nature and Art in William Blake" (February 1939), won a literary award at Columbia University for "the best example of English verse," and published several poems in *Columbia Poetry* and the *New York Times* (June 1939). See Szabo, *In the Dark Before* Dawn, xxii.

25. Lentfoehr, *Words and Silence*, 63–64. See Thurston's "David of Wales," in *Belonging to Borders*, 10–11 in which David is called "Waterman" because of his abstinence from alcohol.

of Fergus" who spent his time praying and sleeping while wrapped in Maedoc's cloak, and the saint's power in stopping a warring king and his army. Notable is the triplet of images that constitute the king's decision to turn back: "No fighting the saints / The Blessed Trinity / Or Maedoc's wonders." Sr. Thérèse Lentfoehr, the earliest interpreter of Merton's poetry, questions whether Merton had access to a real ikon fragment or whether the poem is a symbol of Maedoc's life. She makes special note of the connotative links between images that give the poem its surrealistic pattern by juxtaposing nature and war, reality and miracles.[26] Certainly the Celtic love of nature is evidenced in this poem which grounds its celebration of a trinity of miracles in the "floating stone," "fresh hazel," "wolves," a "green shore," "sunlight in spring rain," "Water and Spirit / Bright wave and flame / at the wood's edge."

A few pages later in this same notebook, Merton tries his hand at another poem—"Merlin and the Deer"—perhaps now more well-known although the poem was not published during his lifetime, nor is it mentioned in Lentfoehr's initial analysis of Merton's poetry.[27] George Kilcourse, however, features the poem in his 1991 article in *The Merton Annual* as an illustration of the process of discovering the "true self."[28] In addition to the poem being based on a real episode of Merton seeing a deer temporarily trapped in the water of the monastery reservoir, what intrigues me is the figure of Merlin.[29] In Welsh mythology Merlin is considered, among other legendary labels, to be a Master of Breath.[30] Breath, that animating principle and portal to higher consciousness, is nature's tool for finding the "self." In Merton's poem, the deer escapes by swimming across the water and disappearing into the trees. Merlin, the Welsh magician wakes up, becomes a "gentle savage / Dressed in leaves" and hums to himself—audible breathing—while saying psalms in the woods. Temporarily sidetracked by the deer episode, Merlin leaves the frigid water of distraction and allows

26. Ibid., 63–64.

27. Merton, "Merlin and the Deer," in *Collected Poems*, 736–37. Because the poem is handwritten in *Working Notebook #14* June 1964, it was presumably composed sometime that year.

28. Kilcourse, "A Shy Wild Deer," 97–109.

29. Merton, *Dancing in the Water of Life*, 158–59.

30. The figure of Merlin has many predecessors, including Myrddin, the "Wild Man of the Woods" who fled to the forest after the battle of Arfderydd (573 CE), lived with animals and was given the gift of prophecy. His legend is identified with the twelfth-century figure of Laioken, and then with Merlin in the fifteenth century.

nature to capture him as a "Willing prisoner of trees and rain." But wait. Is this Merlin or Merton we are talking about? Thomas Merton at this period is transitioning to more extended time in the hermitage in the woods and choosing to be that "prisoner of trees and rain." Yet in the poem he—Merlin/Merton—is not totally alone. The poet mentions the imaginary folks who visit his isolated dwelling with stories about the woods, stories that have no sound and no conclusion. Thus Merlin/Merton magic initiates "Clear fires without smoke / Fumbled prophecies / And Celtic fortunes." With the merging of Merlin/Merton, these woods become one of those "thin places" that reveal secrets of the solitary life, the Otherworld, and— we might add—secrets of the "hidden wholeness" or "true self" deep within the human person.

Despite Merton's obvious joy in this experience of nature and Welsh mythology, his primary interest during the mid-1960s was Celtic monasticism and the Irish hermits in the woods who were writing of the immanence of God revealed in the birds, water, rocks, and trees that comprised their environment. Merton was even toying with creating an Office of Hermits to use for his personal prayer in the hermitage. Some of these early Irish monks went on *peregrinatio*, adrift on the sea, then later founded or settled in a monastery, but some sought the "place of one's resurrection" in the local wild landscape as anchorites or solitary ascetics. Steeped in their Celtic culture of experiencing God in all creation, they were committed to seeking God not just in solitary contemplation but also in their everyday duties, such as copying manuscripts and in their intimate natural environment. Their poetry celebrates the beauty and power of nature in the present moment, as well as their desire for forgiveness from God. They understand the Celtic spirituality of seeing and experiencing creation and redemption—Incarnation and Crucifixion/Resurrection—expressed as one loving action in the Person of Jesus.

In 1964 when he was beginning to immerse himself in Celtic monastic history as described by Nora Chadwick, Robin Flower, and Dom Louis Gougaud, Merton was also reading Kenneth Jackson and Kuno Meyer, the two seminal translators and interpreters of Celtic poetry. Merton's June 2, 1964 journal notation is revealing: "Reading about Celtic monasticism, the hermits, lyric poets, travelers, etc. A new world that has waited until this time to open up." And, indeed, a new world it was! Merton was ecstatic about this new stream of information that supported his growing interest in the solitary life, and in September 1964 put together his own unpublished twenty-three-page "Anthology of Irish Poetry."[31]

Merton's Anthology of Irish Poetry

In looking over Merton's eclectic and sometimes confusing selections in his unpublished Anthology to try to second-guess his choice and arrangement of poems, it is clear that he is using two translations: Kuno Meyer's *Selections from Ancient Irish Poetry* (1911) for the first fourteen poems and, for the next twelve poems, Kenneth Jackson's *Studies in Early Celtic Nature Poetry* (1935). Many of the first poems appear also in Jackson's text, but in a different order and slightly different translation. The final two poems in Merton's collection come from Jackson's *A Celtic Miscellany* (1951).[32]

Merton's eclectic assortment of Irish poems follows a loose thematic pattern: vocation to the hermit life, celebration of the seasons, tribute to sacred places, short quatrains about different subjects that evidently captured his fancy, and a second section entitled: "Ten Celtic Hermit Poems" from Jackson's *Studies*. (Is Merton aware that his homespun numbering actually goes to twelve?) His anthology concludes with "St Columba's Island Hermitage" and "The Hermit" taken from the religion section of Jackson's *A Celtic Miscellany*." A brief overview of Merton's choices will offer the reader a taste of his interests.

Section I

The first selection in Merton's Anthology is "King and Hermit," a long dialogue—really a monologue—in which Marvan renounces his life as a warrior for a "tiny shieling" [isolated hut] in the woods with birds, deer, and the voice of the wind all of which constitute a "Beautiful spot! . . . Without an hour of fighting, without the den of strife / In my house." In a brief response, the King sighs that he would give his "glorious kingship" as well as his inheritance "To be in thy company, my Marvan."[33] While I have

31. Merton, *Collected Essays* 2, 232–54.

32. The earlier book of Jackson includes Irish hermit poetry as well as Welsh gnomic poetry: simple folk wisdom that juxtaposes nature descriptions with philosophical or moral principles. The book is a much broader collection of Irish literature ranging from hero-tales to descriptions, to humor and satire, to elegies, and poems about religion.

33. Merton, "Anthology of Irish Poetry," in *Collected Essays*, 232–34.

identified this text somewhat facilely as a vocation poem, it is more of a rhapsodic soliloquy on the hermit life that presents the hermit as part of the promised hundred-fold here on earth with all the richness of creation "From my good Christ."

Nature is celebrated in the next three poems: summer with its bees, light swallows, peat-bog, and the "timorous, tiny, persistent" lark whose song surpasses "summer-time of delicate hues!"; the second, a lament for the departure of summer with the "sea running high" and an icy temperature that "has caught the wings of birds"; and the third, the cold of winter with its tidal sea, roaming fish, wolves, and "Ice in heaps on every ford—"[34] Tribute to the sea is then highlighted in two poems that function as bookends for the famous "The Monk and His Pet Cat"[35]—quoted in full in a previous chapter of this book. The first nautical poem "Arran" is a celebration of the sea around the island of Ireland as well as the animals and plants of every season that cause the poet to conclude: "Delightful at all times is Arran."[36] The second sea poem, "Colum Cille's Greeting to Ireland" refers to St. Columba, "the Dove." Despite the frequent use of the word "delightful," the text is a lament not only for the Hill of Howth which the sailor, "rowing [his] little coracle" is leaving, but also for his home in Derry, far behind him to the west. Even with his acknowledgement "Grievous is my errand over the main / Travelling to Alba" [England] and tears for his beloved home in Derry, the poet seems to reconcile himself to the beauty of the present moment in the last stanza: "Delightful it is, / The deep-red ocean where the seagulls cry. / As I come from Derry afar, / It is peaceful and it is beautiful."[37]

Next Merton selected two poems about historical figures: "On Angus the Culdee" [hermit or friend of God] who lived in the latter eighth century on the banks of the River Nore and is known for his austerity and love of solitude, and "Alexander the Great" whose friends, standing around his grave, comment on the fleetingness of power and material goods.[38] Then follow five short poems selected from Kuno Meyer's collection of "Quatrains." Merton seems taken with "The Scribe," above whose "lined booklet / The trilling birds chant"; "The Crucifixion," when the "cry of the first bird" heralded the torment of Christ and "the parting of day from night"; "The

34. Ibid., 235–37.

35. Ibid., 239.

36. Ibid., 238.

37. Ibid., 240–41.

38. Ibid., 242.

Blackbird" who, satisfied in his nest, "clinkest no bell" only a "sweet, soft" peaceful" note; and "The Church Bell in the Night" that signals a tryst with God in church preferred by the monk to a tryst "with a foolish woman."[39] In the middle of this group of five quatrains is the famous ninth-century marginalia, "The Pilgrim at Rome," often quoted in discussions of Celtic *peregrinatio* and copied out by Merton in his notes from Nora Chadwick's *The Age of Saints in the Early Celtic Church*: "To go to Rome / Is much of trouble, little of profit: / The King whom thou seekest there, / Unless thou bring Him with thee, thou wilt not find."

Section II

The "Ten Celtic Hermit Poems," that comprise the second half of Merton's Anthology (although Merton has mistakenly included twelve poems) are chosen from Jackson's 1935 translations and continue this theme of finding solace in the woods with the animals and birds for companions, culminating in two longer poems from Jackson's more comprehensive collection, *A Celtic Miscellany*. Poem number "X" in Merton's anthology, "Ah, blackbird, it is well for thee / where thy nest is in the brake," is a translation by Jackson of a quatrain from Meyer's 1928 collection.[40] Was Merton aware of this duplication? Or was he taken with the crispness of Jackson's final line: "melodious, soft, and peaceful is thy call" over Meyer's earlier "sweet, soft, peaceful is thy note"? His preference will probably remain an unanswered question.

One of the two concluding poems, "St. Columba's Island Hermitage," attributed to an unknown twelfth-century author, is also a duplicate of Merton's poem number "VI" (translated by Meyer), but now translated by Jackson and presented, not in quatrains, but in prose couplets with a few minor vocabulary changes. Meyer's opening quatrain reads: "Delightful I think it to be in the bosom of an isle / on the *crest* of a rock, / that I may look there on the *manifold / face* of the sea." Jackson's translation, set in prose lines reads: "Delightful I think it to be in the bosom of an isle, on the *peak* of a rock that I might often see there the *calm* of the sea." The poem applauds the hermit's isolation and adds a list of what else would

39. Ibid., 243. The phrase "foolish woman" is translated by Jackson as "wanton woman."

40. Ibid., 250. Meyer's earlier version reads: "Ah, blackbird, thou are satisfied / Where thy nest is in the bush.

be delightful: "the voice of the wondrous birds," "its mighty whales," "its ebb and its flood-tide," "that I might bewail my many sins," "that I might bless the Lord," "pore on one of my books," "while meditating upon the Kingdom of Heaven," "a while at labour not too heavy." Both versions begin and end with the word "delightful," the conscious literary technique of *epanelepsis*[41] that functions as a kind of "bookend" for rhetorical effect. The speaker in the final poem, "The Hermit," thought to be of eighth- or ninth-century composition, rejoices to be "Alone in my little hut" to pursue various ascetic practices in atonement for sin, concluding: "If of my own I have done wrong at all, through the pride of this world, hear my wail for it all alone, O God!"[42]

While there are many other Irish hermit poems Merton might have chosen for his anthology, these selections bespeak not only his general interest in Celtic monasticism, but also his pleasure in finding a strong resonance between their celebration of and comfort in nature, their longing for contented solitude in a little hut, and Merton's own desire to spend more time in his hermitage. It is as if Merton were seeking a seal of approval for his spiritual leanings and personal prayer in nature. These unknown Irish monks provide that affirmation. Indeed, in July 1965, Merton sent his little anthology to his artist friend Victor Hammer with the comment that "this collection of Irish poems . . . has beautiful possibilities for printing.[43] Merton is taking to heart St. Columbanus's counsel: "Understand creation if you would understand the Creator."[44]

Celtic Imagination and Irish Hermit Poetry

Just who were these Irish hermits and why were they so attractive to Merton? Both Kuno Meyer and Kenneth Jackson agree that because no manuscripts exist from the early days of Celtic literature—comprising six languages and thirteen centuries—"gross misinterpretation" has occurred. Although some critics regard the "Celtic mind as something mysterious, magical, filled with dark broodings over a mighty past . . . in some strange way in direct contact with a mystical supernatural twilight world which they would rarely reveal to the outsider," Jackson is adamant that the Celts

41. Ibid., 249, 253.
42. Ibid., 254, Jackson's translation.
43. Scutchfield and Holbrook, *Letters of Thomas Merton*, 218.
44. Quoted by de Waal, *Celtic Way of Prayer*, 181.

were *not* "given to mysticism or sentimentality . . . their most outstanding characteristic is rather their astonishing power of imagination."[45] If there is any magic in their writing, insists Jackson, it is the magic of the folk tale, for in *this* world the "distinction between natural and supernatural which is the consequence of civilized thought has not yet been clearly drawn."[46] Recall Merton's explanation of imagination quoted in chapter 4: "the creative task of making symbols, joining things together . . . [to] throw new light on each other . . . the imagination is something which enables us to discover unique present meaning in a given moment in our life."[47]

This vivid power of imagination made Irish hermit poetry fresh and original and is evident in the poet's ability to see in new ways—that unique characteristic of the Celtic worldview finely honed in all of the Celtic monks. Robin Flower remarks that "the poets of the old Irish time had always a keen and unaffected delight in the beauty of their country, its hills and rivers, lakes and forests, the cleared plains, and the vast surrounding sea."[48] The tale is recounted of Lady Poverty asking to see the monks' monastery. Gladly they take her to the brow of a hill to witness the vista of the countryside. "This," the monks exclaim, " is our monastery, lady!"[49] The best of the hermit poems, argues Flower, "are all fire and air, praise and prayer and dedication of the heart, touching little upon dogma or miracle, but content and eager with a new joy and a young revelation." [50] As Esther de Waal expresses it in her discussion of Celtic hermits: "They saw the world through eyes washed miraculously clear by continual spiritual exercise; they saw with 'rinsed eyes' . . . They saw with such clarity because the seeing came out of their contemplative vision. And their writing reflects this, with its distinctive freshness and immediacy, its attention to detail."[51] It should not be surprising, de Waal remarks in a footnote, that Merton also has been described as seeing with "rinsed eyes."[52] As a fruit of his own

---

45. Jackson, *Celtic Miscellany*, 12.

46. Ibid., 153.

47. Merton, *Contemplation in a World of Action*, 345.

48. Flower, *Irish Tradition*, 50.

49. Ibid., 64–66.

50. Ibid., 47.

51. De Waal, *Celtic Way of Prayer*, 96; Flower notes that the hermits "brought into that environment an eye washed miraculously clear by a continual spiritual exercise" (*Irish Tradition*, 42).

52. De Waal, *Celtic Way of Prayer*, 221 n. 2.

contemplation, Merton developed a sense of clear vision and the ability to allow every creature its own voice.

Another area of misinterpretation of Celtic nature poetry—including both Irish and Welsh poetry—is the question of emotion. Contrary to critics such as E. Sieper who argues that the Celtic imagination is objective and "infinitely primitive," Jackson maintains that hermit poems are "concerned vitally with the singer's own reaction to his surroundings, not with making a descriptive catalogue [as found in earlier Latin poems] about the various things he sees, but with telling us how he feels about them and how they harmonize or clash with his own particular mood."[53] Using as an example the oft-quoted lines from a hermit-scribe—"Pleasant is the glittering of the sun to-day upon these margins because it flickers so,"—Jackson quotes his mentor Robin Flower as remarking: "It is the emotion, not the sun, that matters here."[54] In short, Jackson and Flower would have us understand that early Celtic poetry is "the work of literary artists, not the crude chant of primitive man."[55]

Kuno Meyer, another scholar of early Celtic poetry, and in particular Irish hermit poetry, offers us valuable insight into the history of the genre. Once the Romans conquered and influenced the life of continental Europe (beginning in 43 CE and lasting into the 400s), native people lost not only their liberty, but their language and vernacular literature as well, so that by the fifth century, most of these cultural expressions were extinct. This, maintains Kuno Meyer, did not happen in Ireland, partly because of its insularity, but primarily because Celtic Christianity can be traced not to Rome, but to Britain and Gaul, and ultimately to Egypt.[56] The sixth century that Nora Chadwick names the "Golden Age of Celtic Saints" is for Meyer the "Golden Age of Irish Civilization"—a time when "vernacular literature received a fresh impulse from the new faith" and "flourishing primitive Christian literature arose."[57] Sadly, despite a rich "oral literature, handed down by many generations of bards and story-tellers . . . first written down in the monasteries," most manuscripts were destroyed by the Viking in-

---

53. Jackson, *Studies in Early Celtic Nature Poetry*, 80. Objectivity was acceptable for Welsh gnomic poetry and seasonal poems, but not for hermit poems.

54. Ibid., 80. Flower translates this as "glint," whereas Jackson chooses "glittering."

55. Ibid., 80–82.

56. Meyer, *Selections from Ancient Irish* Poetry, viii–x. Meyer notes that only three groups left behind some record of their pagan civilization in a vernacular literature—the Irish, the Anglo-Saxons, and Icelanders.

57. Ibid., ix–x.

vasion in the eighth century; however, the contents of many manuscripts attributed to the eleventh century onward—as Meyer, Jackson, Flower, and Chadwick have established—were undoubtedly compiled in the seventh and eighth centuries. Meyer believes that as Irish scholarship advances, "it is not unlikely that fragments of poetry will be found which, from linguistic or internal evidence, may be claimed for the sixth century."[58]

According to Meyer, Irish poets generally did not write epic poetry. Prose was their choice for the hero-narrative. Lyric poetry was written either by professional bards attached to a court or king or by unattached itinerant poets or monks. Their subjects were primarily religious topics, the seasons and nature, but rarely love poems (at least from extant examples). Composed generally in quatrains of four heptasyllabic lines with rhyming couplets that were derived from earlier Latin metres, religious poetry gives us a unique window into the early Celtic Christian church. These poems might feature the "hermit in his lonely cell, the monk at his devotions or at his work of copying in the scriptorium or under the open sky." On occasion they might spotlight the ascetic, praying in the woods, mountains, or on an isolated island.[59] The fervor and discipline of the monk or hermit are central to the text, as illustrated in these two different examples from Robin Flower, the first a prayer, the second a comment on the austerity of "the beehive cells of the monks, built of dry stones."

> Christ keep me safe, Christ guard me lowly,
> Christ bring me to his dwelling high . . .
> . . . This hope I have.

> Cells that freeze,
> The thin pale monks upon their knees,
> Bodies worn with rites austere,
> The falling tear—Heaven's king loves these. [60]

With the development of the anchorite movement in the eighth to tenth centuries (as reconstructed by Robin Flower with his research on the Tallaght and Finglas monasteries), so too was there an "intimate affection for wild life and wild nature, such as we may find elsewhere in Christian sources perhaps only in the story of St. Francis."[61] Thus, Irish hermit po-

---

58. Ibid., xi.

59. Ibid., xii–xiii.

60. Flower, *Irish Tradition*, 49.

61. Jackson, *Celtic Miscellany*, 306.

etry—as an expression of Celtic monasticism—reinforces the ideal of the solitary life: "a little cell in woods and wild," simple fare and an ascetic way of life, harmony with one's surroundings, clarity of vision, and "love and sympathy for wild life" such as the "trilling of birds."[62] Kenneth Jackson makes the important distinction that the third-century BCE Greek poet Theocritus "only listened to birds and noted that their song was pleasant, but the hermits did more than this; they lived so much among the wild creatures that they became almost one with them, almost own brother to them, as it were hardly conscious that there was any distinction of genus."[63] This tendency to celebrate wild life was integral to the tales of early Celtic saints who befriended animals and found in them acceptable companions for praising God.[64] St. Maedoc, for example, is mentioned in the *Lives of the Saints* as meeting a she-wolf who was "piteous, exhausted, starving." Securing some bread and fish from a lad walking along the road, Maedoc "cast them to the wolf" to satisfy her hunger.[65] Likewise, Saint Ciarán of Saighir is said to have met a wild boar who "at first fled in terror," but "becoming calm by God," returned to become his first pupil, cut saplings for his first cell, and joined other animals gathered around Ciarán. One of these pupils, a fox, stole the monk's shoes. At the urging of the wild boar, the fox repented and returned the shoes. This same sympathy with animals is found in the more tame and celebrated ninth-century "The Monk and his Pet Cat," highlighting the "childish craft of mousing" compared to the monk's more challenging "attempt at solving problems of scholarship."[66]

Readers of Merton will recall his fondness for the deer that often appeared at twilight in the meadow outside his hermitage. Between January 1965 and June 1966 there are thirteen references to deer in Merton's journals. They reveal an initial superficial fascination with these mysterious beings—"suddenly realized that there were beings there"—that evolves into deeper insight and reverence.[67] Merton exclaims over the "deerness" he perceives that "reveals to me something essential in myself!"

62. See examples of this poetry in Jackson, *Studies in Early Celtic Nature Poetry*, 96–99.

63. Ibid., 100.

64. Ibid., 103. Jackson makes the point that the hermits had an instinctive need for society and that animals often became the substitute for monastic brothers.

65. Ibid., 101–102.

66. Ibid., 101.

67. Merton, *Dancing in the Water of Life*, 189. See my discussion of the deer in Weis, *Environmental Vision*, 157–65.

> The thing that struck me most: one sees, looking at them directly
> in movement, just what the cave painters saw—something that I
> have never seen in a photograph. It is an awe-inspiring thing—the
> *Mantu* or 'spirit' shown in the running of the deer . . . A contem-
> plative intuition! . . . I could sense the softness of their coat and
> longed to touch them.[68]

Not surprisingly one doe becomes quite used to Merton's pacing back and
forth outside the hermitage while reciting Compline and again, not surprisingly, Merton writes: "Yesterday, Feast of St. Francis. I made a holiday of
it. In the morning (bright and cold) walked through the hollow then to the
long field and in and out the wood where the deer sleep."[69]

In addition to kinship with animals, Celtic texts often express a "strong
personal relationship . . . with God," even speaking of God as "my darling"
or, as in the wish of St. Ita, "to nurse the infant Jesus in her cell." St. Brigid of
Kildare is quoted as professing a desire to "entertain the people of Heaven
at a religious banquet, including 'a great pool of ale' for them to drink."[70]

Because of its island geography, the sea also figures significantly in
Irish hermit poetry which, according to Esther de Waal, is a "place of
revelation."[71] Many of the hermits living among rocks at the edge of the sea
meditated on the mighty ebb and flow of the tides. The voyages of Bran and
of Brendan highlight the danger and mystery of the sea. Kenneth Jackson
is of the opinion that the most remarkable treatment of the sea is found not
in Welsh or British tales, but in Irish poetry, where "the sea was regarded
with genuine delight mingled with terror"—a true experience of the sub-
lime for these "amazingly adventurous sailors."[72] One early poem celebrates
the "fierce exultation in the storm at sea, worthy of the Vikings for whom
tradition says it was composed." The tale of the drowning of Conaing refers
to the "sea's hair," whereas "Columba's Farewell" boasts of a calm sea.[73]

Weather, of course, is important not only to sea-faring people, but also
to all those who live on the land. In Ireland and Wales, weather and fertility
auguries often existed in prose almanacs that foretell the character of the

---

68. Merton, *Dancing in the Water of Life*, 291.

69. Ibid., 300. See my discussion of the deer in Weis, *Environmental Vision*.

70. Jackson, *Celtic Miscellany*, 306, 312–13. Some translations read "a great lake of
beer."

71. De Waal, *Celtic Way of Prayer*, 180.

72. Jackson, *Studies in Early Celtic Nature Poetry*, 91.

73. Ibid., 91–92.

seasons, yet "prognostications in short phrases about the seasons, weather, fertility and prosperity were given in early chant-metre." Jackson offers the noun-adjective or noun-verb formula from a prophecy of Néde as illustrative of a weather chant:

Good tidings (*scela*)
Sea fruitful,
Strand wave-washed,
Woods smile,
Witchcraft flees,
Orchards prosper,
Cornfields flourish,
Bee-swarms abundant,
The world cheerful,
Joyous peace,
Happy summer.[74]

Merton, himself, was fascinated by weather. Often in his journals, he comments on the temperature, rain, sky, or clouds at the beginning or end of an entry. Sometimes he inserts such a comment in the middle of an entry after a discussion of his current reading project. But weather, for Merton is more than a meteorological report; it is a recognition of the very rhythm of his life. In his journal entry for Ash Wednesday, 1963, he confides:

Our mention of the weather . . . [is] perhaps not idle. Perhaps we have a deep and legitimate need to know in our entire being what the day is like, to *see* it and *feel* it, to know how the sky is grey, paler in the south, with patches of blue in the southwest, with snow in the ground, the thermometer at 18, and cold wind making your ears ache. I have a real need to know these things because I myself am part of the weather and part of the climate and part of the place and a day in which I have not shared truly in all this is no day at all. It is certainly part of my life of prayer.[75]

Examining early Celtic poetry, one can sense that in every case, the Celtic poet is adept at presenting not an "elaborate or sustained description" of a scene, but a succession of crisp pictures and precise colorful images with implied emotional overtones, similar to the brush strokes of French impressionism or the subtlety of the Japanese haiku.[76] As Kuno Meyer ex-

74. Ibid., 170.

75. Merton, *Turning Toward the World*, 299–300.

76. Jackson makes the point that there is fine Irish nature poetry as early as the

plains: "The Celts were always quick to take an artistic hint; they avoid the obvious and the commonplace; the half-said thing to them is dearest."[77] Robin Flower evaluates their flair for the precise word this way—which Merton reproduced in his handwritten notes: "The extreme correctness of the Irish way of thought is reflected in the idioms of their language and determines the effect of their literature upon any mind that is at all attuned to distinctions of style." In a similar vein, the elder Cato (234–149 BCE) comments somewhat sharply that the "Celts were distinguished for their aptitude for fighting and for subtle speech. The Irish have well maintained these two characters . . . a sharp and homely brevity of epigrammatic speech eminently calculated for the rapid thrust and return of contentious talk."[78] Nora Chadwick attributes the Celts' special poetic gifts to "the simplicity and integrity of the spiritual elite." They were men who lived a Spartan "life purified from material desires in simple communion with nature."[79] Hence, we see the precision of idioms and concrete images in lines such as this short poem found in Meyer's and Jackson's parallel translations, which appear in the first half of Merton's anthology as "The Blackbird" and in the second half identified as number "X":

Ah, blackbird, thou art satisfied	Ah, blackbird, it is well for thee
Where thy nest is in the bush;	where thy nest is in the brake;
Hermit that clinkest no bell	hermit that dost not clang a bell
Sweet, soft, peaceful is thy note.	melodious, soft, and peaceful is thy call.[80]

In each translation, bird and hermit are synonymous, yet different in that the bird's "bell" is a gentle, natural sound in sharp contrast to the man-made bell ("clinkest" versus "clang") intended to remind the hermit of his monastic obligations. For the Celtic monk, the striking of the bell—done only at the abbot's direction—signaled both a heavenly call to all earth-dwellers as well as a promise of Divine fidelity as we see in this example from Flower.[81]

---

ninth century which tends to be impressionistic; however, there are no early Welsh nature poems—their writing tends to be sententious and epigrammatic. See *Studies in Early Celtic Nature* Poetry, 177.

77. Meyer, *Selections from Ancient Irish Poetry*, xiii.

78. Flower, *Irish Tradition*, 110; Merton, *Working Notebook #48*.

79. Chadwick, *Age of Saints*, 165.

80. Merton, "Anthology of Irish Poetry," 243, 250.

81. Flower, *Irish Tradition*, 49, originally from *Archiv fur celticshe lexikographie*, iii, 233.

The clear-voiced bell
On chill wild night God's hours doth tell;
Rather in it I'll put my trust
Than in a wanton woman's lust.

Consider, too, this example, labeled "VII" in Merton's anthology:

There is here above the brotherhood
a bright tall glossy yew;
the melodious bell sends out a clear keen note.
in St. Columba's church.[82]

In this second poem, both tree and bell can be seen or heard on high, and both represent an implied sacred reality. As Esther de Waal reminds us: Our ancestors did not regard trees as mere natural objects; rather they were "majestic signs of the connectedness of the heaven and the earth."[83] One is reminded also of Merton's description of his day in the hermitage, *Day of a Stranger*, written in May 1965, that also celebrates the brotherhood with nature and deep prayer of his hermit life:

I know there are trees here. I know there are birds here. I know the birds in fact very well, for there are precise pairs of birds (two each of fifteen or twenty species) living in the immediate area of my cabin. I share this particular place with them: we form an ecological balance. This harmony gives the idea of "place" a new configuration.[84]

It is this intimate connection with nature that poets like David Whyte and John O'Donohue, among other aficionados of Celtic studies, celebrate as a veritable conversation among all the creatures and elements: bird, tree, water, rock, vegetation, and soil.[85] If matter and spirit interpenetrate one another, there is a kinship to be recognized, acknowledged, and acclaimed.

Kinship with particular birds is often cited in Merton's journals and appears frequently as well in early Celtic poetry and Irish hermit poetry. A cursory glance at the poetic selections included in Merton's "Anthology" offers a broad list of winged creatures: lark, blackbird, ousel, cuckoo, herons, seagulls, wild goose. In Celtic lore, there are many stories of birds

---

82. Merton, "Anthology of Irish Poetry," 250.

83. De Waal, *Celtic Way of Prayer*, 148.

84. Merton, *Day of a Stranger*, 33.

85. O'Donohue, "Celtic Pilgrimage with John O'Donohue." See also Hempstead-Milton, "Emblems of Birds," 16–24.

and humans sharing praise of God, even oral reports of bards wearing bird feathers.[86] To this end Robin Flower maintains that "hermit poetry is never so lovely as when it has to tell of the bird's song that cheered the scribe at his meticulous labours and the anchorite at his long prayers and vigils." As illustration, Flower offers this delightful piece:

> The tiny bird
> Whose call I heard
> I marked his yellow bill;
> The ousel's glee
> Above Lough Lee
> Shakes golden branches still.[87]

Birds were also significant in early Celtic culture as a way of marking time. As far back as Hesiod's almanac (700 BCE) farmers knew that the first cry of the cuckoo marked the beginning of a season. Early bird-song calendars, as both Flower and Jackson agree, suggest a shared tradition between the English and the Irish, because "the passing of the seasons was noted in the almanac literature of these islands at an early period."[88] Merton copies into *Working Notebook #14* Jackson's reference to bird song calendars and adds his own comment about the Calendar of Pseudo-Bede from the Durham Manuscript in *PL* [*Patrologia Latina*] that February 11 or 12 was the "day when the birds begin to sing" and they cease on June 17.[89] The *Navigatio Sancti Brendani* also picks up on this bird imagery. The welcoming monks on one island remain in their cells after Compline until cockcrow; on another island, the birds join in singing the office with them, answering the call to prayer—"Thou shalt open my lips, O Lord"—with the response "Praise the Lord, all his angels; praise him, all his virtues."[90] Merton, too, often refers to the birds as accompanying his recitation of the Divine Office, heralding the dawn of day, and teaching him the value of practicing contemplation.[91] Certainly these references to birds are more than simple

---

86. De Waal, *Celtic Way of Prayer*, 14.

87. Flower, *Irish Tradition*, 61, from *Irische Texts*, iii, 99.

88. Jackson, *Studies in Early Celtic Nature Poetry*, 165–66.

89. Merton, *Working Notebook #14*.

90. See Kingsley, *The Hermits*, chapter 10, "The Celtic Hermits," in which he recounts at length the "Navigation of St. Brendan," based on the French version of the tale.

91. Merton, *Entering the Silence*, 408. When Merton observes a hawk snatching a starling, he remarks that he wishes he knew his business of contemplation as well as the hawk knows his. See my discussion of this event in Weis, *Environmental Vision*, 53–55.

simpatico. They support an understanding of the Celtic worldview and celebration of the elements: rock, sea, earth, fire, seasons, and annual patterns.[92] They exemplify the more modern notion put forth by paleontologist Teilhard de Chardin of "the breathing together of all things."[93] In *Working Notebook #15* dated 1965–August 1966, Merton sketches ideas for, among other things, a long anti-poem, *Cables to the Ace*—a concise reflection that effectively becomes his own marginalia, pulling together the beauty of nature, the solitude of the hermit, and the prayer of the contemplative:

> My worship is a blue sky and ten thousand
> crickets in the deep wet grass of the field.
> My vow is the silence under their
> Sound. I support the woodpecker & the dove.
> Together we learn the norms. The plowed & planted field
> says: *it is my turn*. And several of us
> begin to sing.[94]

The bottom line, as Donald Allchin and Esther de Waal have said repeatedly, is that Celtic poetry was in a very real and deep sense an act of praise, bringing the "whole world together as participants in the singing of one great hymn of praise. The hermit who might seem to be most alone in his or her cell praying the canonical hours and singing the Psalms is least alone."[95] Kenneth Jackson makes the point that bird songs are an apt example of the distinction between the Greek poets and the Celtic hermits: distance versus emotional engagement. "The Greeks stopped short of the wilderness. The hermits did not; they were 'Simple Lifers' who really did live the simple life, and that in its simplest form." The Celtic "hermits sought spiritual purity in nature . . . Yet the ultimate significance of the hermit's relationship with nature is something that transcends both nature and hermit alike."[96] Certainly Merton's scribbled notation above is a prime example of Jackson's point. It is no wonder that Thomas Merton copies this Jackson quotation into his *Working Notebook #14* along with this succeeding passage:

92. De Waal, *Celtic Way of Prayer*, x.

93. Teilhard, quoted in ibid., xv.

94. Merton, *Working Notebook #15*.

95. De Waal, *Celtic Way of Prayer*, 199.

96. Jackson, *Studies in Early Celtic Nature Poetry*, 108.

The woodland birds might sing to him around his cell, but through it all, rarely expressed, always implicit, is the understanding that the bird and hermit are joining together in an act of worship; to him the very existence of nature was a song of praise in which he himself took part by entering into harmony with nature.[97]

Jackson's subsequent sentence, however, Merton does *not* copy. Jackson writes: "It was from this harmony with nature, this all-perceiving contemplation of it, that the Irish hermits reached to a more perfect unison with God." Perhaps this insight is too obvious to Merton—from both his study and his personal experience of prayer. For good measure, however, Merton copies into his notebook this synopsis from Jackson: "The solitary hermitage in the wilderness, the life of ascetic purity and humble piety, the spare diet of herbs and water, and the companionship of wild creatures, are the distinguishing marks of the Irish hermit poetry."[98] Jackson captures it all: solitude, asceticism of spirit and diet, kinship with creatures.

Merton certainly could relate to this experience, and had several years earlier offered a startling description of his interaction with creation in solitude. In his journal entry for June 5, 1960, Pentecost, he writes: "The other day (Thursday)—the *full meaning* of lauds, and against the background of waking birds and sunrise." He goes on to itemize the genesis of the creatures and the dawn: the bullfrog who some mornings "says Om," the whippoorwill, sometimes "close," sometimes "in the distance," and "the first chirps of the waking birds—*le point vierge* [the virgin point] of the dawn, a moment of awe and inexpressible innocence, when the Father in silence opens their eyes and they speak to Him, wondering if it is time to 'be' And He tells them 'Yes.'" Merton's editorial comment after this list of waking is also enlightening: "With my hair almost on end and the eyes of the soul wide open I am present, without knowing it at all, in this unspeakable Paradise, and I behold this secret, this wide open secret which is there for everyone, free, and no one pays any attention."[99]

Certainly this harmony with nature which enabled Celtic hermits to experience a deeper and deeper communion with the Divine was, for Merton, the essence of hermit spirituality. No wonder the writings of the

97. Ibid., 108–9.

98. Ibid., 103.

99. Merton, *Turning Toward the World,* 7 and in a revised version in *Conjectures of a Guilty Bystander,* 131–32. See my discussion of this event in Weis, *Environmental Vision,* 58–63.

Celtic hermits, and especially the poetry of the Irish hermits, captured his attention. Despite the separation of centuries, the Celts and Merton were coming from the same worldview, the same mystical experience, and seeking the same union with the Divine. Whether at sea in a fragile *currach*, wandering the craggy terrain, or choosing exile in a woodland hut, these monks had discovered a way to meet the challenge of St. Brendan's *peregrinatio*—learning how to live in time yet in touch with eternity. In short, they had discovered how to live out of a "transfigured centre."

6

Conclusion:
A New World Opening Up

And so, the question: Why did Thomas Merton spend so much time during the last four years of his life researching, studying, reading, taking notes on early Celtic monasticism, and collecting examples of Irish hermit poetry? What was the motivation? Judging from calendar events, it might have been the death of family members and a desire to reclaim his Welsh heritage; it might have been his meeting and subsequent friendship with A. M. (Donald) Allchin; it might have been his correspondence with Professor Nora Chadwick and his enthusiasm for the notion of *peregrinatio*; it might have been his research and interest in Eastern and Syrian monasticism and its unique expression in Irish monasticism. In reality, it might have been all of the above. What we can say is that Merton's spiritual journey was enriched by these individual experiences that became a confluence of spiritual energy for his final years.

While there is probably no single definitive answer to the question of motivation, I continue to be intrigued by Merton's June 2, 1964 journal entry: "Reading about Celtic monasticism, the hermits, lyric poets, travelers, etc. A new world that has waited until this time to open up."[1] Entries in Merton's journal for the previous months of 1964 indicate a certain restlessness and dissatisfaction with his prayer, a longing for more solitude, a desire to visit a Cistercian monastery in Wales, distress over the "excess of my activity," and the "wrong kind of talking."[2] But June 2 offers a turning point in his spiritual edginess. The attraction of Celtic monasticism was giving Merton a new world to explore with nourishment for his own interior pilgrimage. Perhaps the words of the Irish monk Brendan of Birr (d. 572)—not to be

1. Merton, *Dancing in the Water of Life*, 107.
2. Ibid. See entries on pages 100, 103, 106.

confused with Brendan the Navigator of Clonfort—capture what is inherent in this moment of grace for Merton: "If you become Christ's, you will stumble upon wonder upon wonder and every one of them true."[3]

I want to suggest that Merton's keen interest in all things Celtic is the result of his absolute commitment to Christ and his stumbling "upon wonder upon wonder" and finding "every one of them true"— not the stumbling of a disoriented or semi-conscious person, but the serendipitous and unasked for graces that affirm Merton's commitment to live his monastic vocation entirely for Christ. Don't we often say: "Timing is everything."

Surely time is a critical factor in everyone's spiritual growth, and there are many significant moments of timing in Merton's growth—a succession of grace-full stumblings upon wonders. His trip to Cuba and visit to the shrine of Our Lady of Cobre immersed Merton in a culture of joy, provided inspiration for a poem, and evoked a moment of deep *Creo in Dios*—an overwhelming awareness of God, he writes, that "struck me like a thunderclap."[4] Likewise his epiphanic moment at Fourth and Walnut Streets in Louisville is a well-known turning point of "waking from a dream of separateness" and monastic distance to recognize God's incarnation in humanity. In a burst of spiritual insight, Merton accepts each person crossing the busy street as a brother and sister "shining like the sun."[5] Similarly, in the last weeks of his life, Merton's experience of the Great Buddhas at Polonnaruwa reveals a "clarity as if exploding from the rocks themselves" and he finds himself "beyond the shadow and the disguise."[6] Each of these experiences is a graced moment of "wonder" that shapes his thinking and prayer. But the years of the 1960s held other, not so well-known, moments of wonder. When Merton is drawn to his Welsh heritage and greater knowledge of Celtic culture and monasticism through his connection with Donald Allchin and Nora Chadwick, he is being lured into a yet deeper (or higher) level of intellectual and spiritual consciousness.

Merton's personal interest in his ancestry will always be something of a curiosity since his Welsh blood is from the Bird side of the family—his father's grandmother who was one-half Welsh and one-half Scottish—not

3. Quoted in Adam, *Open Gate*, 2. It is believed that this Brendan was an early Irish monk and friend of St. Columba who studied at Clonard monastery, was one of the twelve Apostles of Ireland, and founded the monastery at Birr c. 540. This Brendan is noted for his hospitality, sanctity, spirituality, and intuitive judgment of character.

4. Merton, *Seven Storey Mountain*, 278–85.

5. Merton, *Conjectures*, 142.

6. Merton, *Other Side of the Mountain*, 323.

exactly a strong lineage, yet Merton clung to this legacy, not only for the influence of the physiognomy ("the look, the grin, the brow") he shared with that lineage, but also for the identification and stability it apparently offered him. Understandably then, with overtones of *hiraeth* [homesickness for the native soil], "angel father mother Wales" becomes the prow or figurehead—in "Prologue: The Endless Inscription"—for *The Geography of Lograire*, that guides him on a poetic *peregrinatio* to the four points of the cosmos. His friendship with Donald Allchin opens for Merton the delights of the Welsh imagination, and his correspondence with Nora Chadwick exposes him to Celtic monasticism and Brendan's voyage—an added academic component to his fascination with the Celts.

Nevertheless, what must be emphasized is that these moments of wonder, significant as they are, do not exist in a vacuum. And this is a critical point: encounter with Celtic culture and monasticism bears fruit precisely because of the context or predisposition in which the encounter takes place. This predisposition is Merton's ongoing intellectual and spiritual development.

Previous years of prolonged study, personal contemplation, and carefully researched conferences presented to the Trappist community provide both the foundation and vitality for what Merton refers to as "a new world that has waited until this time to open up." Merton's journal reveals some interesting details about that opening up. During the interval between March and September of 1964, while he was longing for more solitude, Merton was engaged in many and various nourishing activities: meeting with D. T. Suzuki in New York City and spending time at the Columbia University library reading the Celtic Rule of Tallaght. During that same interval, he was finishing reading Adamnán's *Life of St. Columba*—which deeply moved him[7] —and gratefully receiving a copy of *Navigatio Sancti Brendani* from the Boston College Library, finishing his essay "From Pilgrimage to Crusade," writing the Preface for *Russian Mystics* by Sergius Bolshakoff, reading Celtic poems selected by Kenneth Jackson, discovering additional poems about Brendan, including W. H. Auden's *The Enchafèd Flood* [a series of lectures about the sea that Merton considers valuable background for the Brendan tale], reading books recommended by Nora Chadwick, and drawing Celtic crosses on the blackboard for the delight of the novices.[8] All of these diverse activities found root in the fecund

7. Merton, *Dancing in the Water of Life*, 126.
8. Ibid., 100–142.

soil of his agile intellect already grounded in Eastern and Western mystical and theological thought. This predisposition that cultivated a unique receptiveness to Celtic spirituality bears closer examination.

Tracing the Context and Connections

Oliver Davies in his comparative study of Merton and Meister Eckhart makes the point that Merton is a paradigmatic spiritual figure for his age primarily because he steeped himself in the teaching of the Fathers, especially Maximus the Confessor, read most of the Russian thinkers, and explored monastic forms of Asian religions.[9] Davies is not alone in his appreciation of Merton's diverse background. Christopher Pramuk in *Sophia: The Hidden Christ of Thomas Merton* cites similar influences on Merton's thinking—influences, he argues, that find full flowering in Merton's prose poem *Hagia Sophia*, a "quintessential hermit poem," and "classic of modern Christian mysticism."[10]

Drawing from Pramuk's analysis, I want to suggest that four areas of interest—the theology of the Eastern theologians with their devotion to *theoria physike*, Russian sophiology and literature, the philosophy of Herakleitos, and the principles of Zen—created a sound foundation and context for Merton's new-found enthusiasm for Celtic culture and monasticism.

Early Christian Mysticism

Integral to this context is Thomas Merton's series of classes on Christian Mysticism, given to the recently ordained Trappist priests during Spring of 1961 and continuing somewhat informally into September of that year.[11] Trying to offer them an overview of the great Eastern and Western mystic tradition, Merton spent considerable time discussing the importance of *theoria physike* (natural contemplation), first formulated in the fourth century by Evagrius, and in the seventh century fleshed out by Maximus the Confessor and revered by fourteenth-century mystics, especially Meister Eckhart. Evagrius, a monk in Egypt, regarded nature as "letters" written to

9. Davies, "Thomas Merton and Meister Eckhart," 16.

10. I am grateful for the insight gained from Pramuk's scholarship, especially chapter 4, "The Dawn of Wisdom," *Sophia*, 131–76.

11. Merton, *Introduction to Christian Mysticism*, xi.

human beings by God.[12] Building on this insight, Maximus the Confessor (d. 622) defined *theoria physike* as that "mysterious, silent revelation of God in His cosmos and in the *oikonomia* [incarnation history] as well as in our own lives."[13] Regarded as the "Father of Byzantine mysticism," Maximus was articulate in identifying the *logoi* of created things, not as material substance, but as the spiritual center—in Scripture, in nature, and in human beings. In Merton's words, *theoria physike* is a "vision of the world" that "encounters God walking in the Garden" that realizes "that God has come again alive with us in our own home, and that in the end, He will raise [to] life not only our own bodies but the created universe to a divine and transfigured life."[14] Merton was equally articulate in noting Maximus' theology of creativity, through which God hands over to us a participation in and responsibility for making and restoring harmony in the cosmos. As examples of this cooperative creativity, Merton mentions to the novices the simplicity and fine lines of Shaker furniture and barns that "fit in," abstract art, and Zen calligraphy. He takes delight in sharing with them Maximus's vivid—and perhaps startling—imagery quoted by Hans von Balthasar: "The whole world is a GAME OF GOD. As one amuses children with flowers and bright colored clothes and then gets them later used to more serious games, literary studies, so God raises us up first of all by the great game of nature, then by the Scriptures [with their poetic symbols]. Beyond the symbols of Scripture is the Word."[15]

Maximus's idea of the Divinity reminds us that God is not a "What" but a "Who." How like the final lines in *New Seeds of Contemplation* (which he was revising about this same time) in which Merton reminds us how "the Lord plays and diverts Himself in the garden of His creation"—this God who invites us to "follow Him in His mysterious, cosmic dance . . . to forget ourselves on purpose, cast our awful solemnity to the winds and join in the general dance."[16] For sure, Merton's research into the history of mysticism is the source of much of his wisdom in books he is writing during this period: *The New Man*, and *New Seeds of Contemplation*.

Imagine the explosion of ideas that must have been flaring up in Merton's mind—a convergence of spiritual truths from widely diverse sources.

12. Stewart, *Cassian the Monk*, 52.

13. Merton, *Introduction to Christian Mysticism*, 123–24.

14. Merton, "Notes and Sentences," E.1, 89.

15. Merton, *Introduction to Christian Mysticism*, 132.

16. Merton, *New Seeds of Contemplation*, 296–97.

Celtic monasticism, also strongly indebted to Evagrius and Maximus, celebrates the outpouring of God into the cosmos via creation and the Incarnation. Each creature—and that certainly includes humans—shares in the divinity of God. We come from the "eternal womb of God."[17] Furthermore, Celtic spirituality invites our participation in God's energy through the various fine arts. How manifest, then, is the Divine Presence in Celtic *trequetra* drawings, illuminated manuscripts, knots and designs, and those carved high crosses that bring the dynamic story of Christianity to life on motionless stone! Merton captures something of this excitement in his discussion of Irish monasticism in Section II of his essay, "From Pilgrimage to Crusade." He writes that the Irish monk exhibited an acute

> sense of ontological and spiritual dialogue between man and creation in which spiritual and bodily realities interweave and interlace themselves like manuscript illuminations in the Book of Kells. This resulted in an astonishing spiritual creativity . . . [His] vocation was to mystery and growth, to liberty and abandonment to God, in self-commitment to the apparent irrationality of the winds and the seas, in witness to the wisdom of God the Father and Lord of the elements. Better perhaps than the Greeks, some of the Celtic monks arrived at the purity of that *theoria physike* which sees God not in the essences or *logoi* of things but in a hierophanic cosmos; hence the marvelous vernacular nature poetry of the sixth and seventh-century Celtic hermits.[18]

Soon after Merton's extended course on Christian mysticism, he had his first contact with Donald Allchin whose interest in Eastern Orthodoxy complemented in a significant way Merton's reading of Cassian and the Greek Fathers. Allchin affirmed Merton's perspective on *theoria physike* and the significance of Maximus's and fourteenth-century Gregory Palamas's teaching that an experience of God which is rooted in the senses is a spiritual reality that transforms the body.[19] There is no distinction or separation between the sacred and the secular. It is precisely through the body that "we are able to perceive the light of God shining out in that creation, and thus we are able . . . to offer the praise of all creation to almighty God." How like the Celtic belief in the sacredness of creation, the unity of matter and spirit, and "the silence on fire" Merton had celebrated in an earlier

17. Newell, *Christ of the Celts*, 57.

18. Merton, "From Pilgrimage to Crusade," 191–92.

19. Allchin, "Worship of the Whole Creation," 195.

poem. How like the *haecceitas* of Duns Scotus who recognized the unique *this-ness* of each creature and kinship of each mountain, tree, and spring of water—each of which gives praise to God. How like the holy giddiness of the ancient Celt—and by extension Merton himself—who was "very much a God-intoxicated man whose life was embraced on all sides by the Divine Being. But this presence was always mediated through some finite, this-worldly reality, so that it would be difficult to imagine a spirituality more down to earth than this one.[20]

Russian Theological and Literary Writers

Donald Allchin was also a well-known expert in nineteenth-and twentieth-century Russian Orthodox theology and was able to fill in some of its fine points for Merton because Allchin knew personally some members of the Russian Orthodox theological community exiled in Paris. Allchin satisfied Merton's thirst for information and deeper understanding of sophianic (Wisdom) consciousness as explored by Sergei Bulgakov, N. A. Berdyaev, Paul Evdokimov, and Vladimir Lossky. Despite the differences in the theology of Bulgakov and Berdyaev (the former, according to Allchin, more speculative and daring in his explanation of divine wisdom, the later more of a free religious thinker) Allchin believed that Merton was "bearing witness to some of the thoughts they shared" as they became more integral to his own thinking in later years.[21] As early as 1957 Merton considered the Russian writings to be responsive to the "challenge of the image of Proverbs where Wisdom is 'playing in the world' before the face of the Creator." He valued their capacity to recognize human life as a "powerful Pentecost" and our vocation "to offer the cosmos to the Father, by the power of the Spirit, in the Glory of the Word."[22]

Both Bulgakov and Berdyaev, notes Allchin, shared three important elements in their teaching that resonated with Merton: a cosmic vocation of humankind that we cannot discount; a vocation to a life of prayer, worship, and contemplation that is to be "lived on behalf of creation in a Trinitarian

20. Macquarrie, *Paths in Spirituality*, 7. This phrase has been applied to Merton by Pearson in "Sentinels," 4.

21. Allchin, "Our Lives, A Powerful Pentecost," 37–38. This essay was originally a lecture on the occasion of the opening of the new Thomas Merton Center in the W. L. Brown Library of Bellarmine University, Louisville, KY, October 10, 1997.

22. Merton, *Search for Solitude*, 86.

context," that is, a call to offer all things to the Father, through the life-giving death of the Son, in the transforming power of the Spirit; and thirdly, an invitation to become co-creators with the Spirit who is the Creator of life.[23] Evdokimov's theology, in particular, extolled the sanctity of the natural world and regarded creation and Incarnation as expressions of the Divine Eros that "brings forth the cosmos from chaos."[24] Lossky's book on Eckhart—which Merton read in July 1961—moved him to acknowledge how "it is for me personally a book of immense and providential importance, because . . . I am right in the middle of the most fundamental intuition of unknowing which was the first source of my faith and which ever since has been my whole life.[25] The Russian sophiologists' contributions to theology, Merton believed, had "given us a way of reconciling two contrasting strands in the Christian tradition: the contemplative or mystical on the one side, and the prophetic or eschatological on the other."[26]

Merton at this time was also in correspondence with Boris Pasternak, even writing a review essay of his seminal novel *Dr. Zhivago* in which Merton viewed Pasternak as a cosmic mystic "plunged fully into the midstream of the lost tradition" of *theoria physike* of the Greek Fathers.[27] The significance of Pasternak and his Russian novel, wrote Merton, is its "creative symbolism, the power of imagination and of intuition, the glory of liturgy, and the fire of contemplation."[28] Pasternak, he believed, was "a writer of great power, a man of new and original vision, whose work . . . creates a whole new world."[29] High praise for a dissident impelled by love and spiritual values to rise above the narrow and stifling confinement of Soviet ideology.

I can only imagine how Merton's mind must have been swirling with stimulating new ideas, observing not only the power of imagination but

23. Allchin, "Our Lives, a Powerful Pentecost," 37–38.

24. Pramuk, *Sophia*, 160.

25. Merton, *Hidden Ground of Love*, 344, quoted by Allchin, "Our Lives, a Powerful Pentecost," 46.

26. Allchin, "Our Lives, a Powerful Pentecost," 48. Allchin suggests that Merton's reading of the Russian sophiologists was an important element in his "growth into maturity."

27. Merton, *Literary Essays*, 46. This review was first published in *Jubilee*, July 1959 and together with a second theological critique published in *Thought*, November 1959, and in 1960 in *Disputed Questions*.

28. Merton, *Literary Essays*, 56.

29. Ibid., 43–44.

also the fire of contemplation in Pasternak and the Russian sophiologists. Then, with his extensive reading in Celtic monasticism, Merton was realizing that many of these same characteristics informed the prayer and practice of the early Celtic monks. Moreover, the explanation of Incarnation and Trinity attributed to the Greek Fathers and the Russian Orthodox theologians resonated with the Celtic understanding and celebration of Trinity. Both East and West were engaged in offering praise to the Community of Persons responsible for creating, saving, and sanctifying us. Both East and West, with their gifts of mysticism and distinctness, were living out—to use Esther de Waal's term—a "creation-filled" spirituality. What an awesome correlation of belief and praxis. In 1957 Merton wrote in his journal that he desired to unite in himself the best of the East and West:

> If I can unite *in myself*, in my own spiritual life, the thought of the East and the West, of the Greek and Latin Fathers, I will create in myself a reunion of the divided Church, and from that unity in myself can come the exterior and visible unity of the Church. For, if we want to bring together East and West, we cannot do it by imposing one upon the other. We must contain both in ourselves and transcend them both in Christ.[30]

It seems to me that after encountering the Russians and then the Celts, Merton's early desire was not only affirmed but also accomplished. He was discovering how to integrate the best each culture had to offer. Yet there were two additional facets to this unique predisposition for Celtic spirituality: Herakleitos and Zen Buddhism.

Herakleitos and the Fire Within

Merton in the early 1960s was writing about Herakleitos, whom Christian writers such as Clement of Alexandria dubbed the "Saint of pre-Christian paganism," and whose belief in the "dynamic principle of harmony-in-conflict" urges us to "awaken to the fire that is within."[31] In *The Behavior of Titans* (1961) Merton celebrated the divine energy at play in nature that is ours for the asking—not an abstract force, but the "intuition of the One fire flame[ing] out to an awareness of divine presence in all persons and

---

30. Merton, *Search for Solitude*, 87.
31. Merton, *Behavior of Titans*, 77.

things."[32] Herakleitos—and Merton's tribute to him—offers us a vision of the gratuitous unity-in-multiplicity that is present in the cosmos. This inner fire is something the early Celts understood. Duns Scotus celebrated this inner fire in his "intuition of patterns and harmonies" in nature, and poet Gerard Manley Hopkins, through his concept of "inscape," saluted its dynamic presence in the world. Influenced by these writers and by his own deepening spirituality, Merton saw in those around him—as did Hopkins—how "Christ plays in ten thousand places," and how, in the woods, nature would "flame out like shining from shook foil."[33]

This understanding is close to ninth-century Irish theologian Eriugena's teaching of creation as a theophany of God and Maximus's explanation of the uncreated energies of God holding all creation together. This understanding of nature resonates with the Celtic hermit's literary and aesthetic spontaneity that found outlet in both prayer and poetry and echoes Kenneth Jackson's insight that "bird and hermit are joining together in an act of worship."[34] Such openness to the eternal-here-and-now was totally consistent with Merton's own monastic experience, his extended time in his hermitage in the woods, and his growing sense of responsibility for creation.[35]

The Influence of Zen

A fourth significant context to support Merton's fascination with Celtic spirituality was his long-time study of Zen and his correspondence and subsequent meeting with D. T. Suzuki. Although he had been in contact with Suzuki as far back as the 1950s, Merton's 1964 meeting with him revealed the striking resonance between Buddhist and Christian mysticism. Since the key to Buddhism is emptiness (*sunyata*) and mindfulness—becoming awake to an experience of new consciousness—Merton could easily draw lines of comparison with St. Paul's admonition to "Let the same

32. Pramuk, *Sophia*, 141. See his discussion of Herakleitos, pages 137–42.

33. "As kingfishers catch fire," and "God's Grandeur," in Hopkins, *Poems of Gerard Manley Hopkins*, 90, 66.

34. Jackson, *Studies in Early Celtic Nature Poetry*, 108–9, quoted by Merton in *Working Notebook #14*.

35. See my discussion of Merton's growing ecological sensitivity in Weis, *Environmental Vision*, 126–56.

mind be in you which was also in Christ Jesus . . . who emptied himself."[36] It was natural for Merton to recognize the reverberations with the writings of mystics such as Meister Eckhart who reminds us that "We love God with His own love; awareness of it deifies us."[37] Suzuki, for his part, embraced the clarifications of Eckhart and was eager to compare "Jesus' beatitude of poverty of spirit, so dear to ancient and Eastern Christian monasticism, to the Zen realization of Emptiness that breaks through when the mind or heart is emptied of all things."[38] Paradoxically, Zen emptiness "is not an emptiness of nothing, but the emptiness of fullness."[39] In Eckhart's words, which Suzuki thought captured the reality, there is no hole to be filled by God; rather, the monk experiences a "breaking through" to "find God and I are the same."[40] The monk's emptiness—which is also an "openness"—initiates a "crossing over to the shore of perfection" expressed in a "going out of oneself" in charity and creative action.[41]

How near this notion of "crossing over" is to the Celtic challenge of *trasna*, the crossing place for pilgrims at a gap in the rocky cliffs faced with the decision to go back to security or forward into the unknown. Merton expresses something of this experience of being at the "crossing place" in his February 18, 1964 journal entry. He has been reading Dom André Louf's confidential and unpublished study of *Christian Eremitism* that argues for "sustained faithfulness" as a criterion for a monk choosing solitude. Sadly, Merton acknowledges on this twenty-second anniversary of reception of the Trappist habit that he has been confused at times, and that as he looks back, despite God's mercy and grace, he has wallowed in "years of false fervor, asceticism, intransigence, intolerance." His choice is to return to "a little of the asceticism . . . without the intolerance and uncharity" and to "find refuge in the psalms, in the chanted office, the Liturgy."[42] For sure, this variation of *peregrinatio* requires that Zen emptying of hopes, plans, and dreams yet mindfulness of the present moment. This variation of *peregrinatio* requires an openness and spirit of adventure so evident in the Celtic mindset. Merton's moment of *trasna* is akin to Brendan's decision to

---

36. Phil 2: 5–11, NRSV; Merton, *Zen and the Birds of Appetite*, 74.

37. Merton, *Zen and the Birds of Appetite*, 75.

38. Ibid., 108–9, quoted by Pramuk, *Sophia*, 166.

39. Ibid., 134, quoted by Pramuk, *Sophia*, 168.

40. Ibid., 114, quoted by Pramuk, *Sophia*, 168.

41. Ibid., 114.

42. Merton, *Dancing in the Water of Life*, 77–80.

voyage into the unknown and like the white martyrdom of the monastic *peregrinatio* travel "to a mysterious, unknown, but divinely appointed place, which was to be the place of the monk's ultimate meeting with God."[43]

The concept of emptying oneself (*sunyata* in Zen and *kenosis* in Christianity) was particularly attractive to Merton. Earlier in a March 25, 1960 journal entry—on the feast of the Annunciation—he explored the ramifications of this emptying:

> In emptying Himself to come into the world, God has not simply kept in reserve, in a safe place, His reality and manifested a kind of shadow or symbol of Himself. He has emptied Himself and is *all* in Christ . . . Christ is not simply the tip of the little finger of the Godhead, moving in the world, easily withdrawn, never threatened, never really risking anything. God has acted and given Himself totally, without division, in the Incarnation. He has become not only one of us but even our very selves.[44]

Merton's fascination with Celtic thought and Celtic monasticism—grounded in his knowledge of Eastern thought—is a significant next step in his physical and spiritual *peregrinatio*, which actually began long before his entrance into the monastery at Gethsemani. To be sure, Merton's pilgrimage is not an event, but an evolution—an evolution of action and spirit that embraced the asceticism of the Desert Fathers and Mothers, Greek philosophy, the Eastern Fathers of the church, the medieval mystics, Western monasticism, Russian orthodoxy, and Zen. When Merton first became acquainted with Celtic spirituality, it "got its hooks" into him for obvious genealogical reasons. But with more study and the voracious reading program he created for himself, Merton discovered not *new* theology, but an *old* theology rooted in the principles of Creation and Incarnation. This evolving Merton—who for so long had been searching for a home—found himself in the writings of Celtic monasticism and its challenge to live out of a "transfigured centre."

In the play *Julius Caesar*, Shakespeare has Brutus mouth an extended metaphor about the need to recognize the *kairos* experience—that opportune moment beyond chronological time in which significant and unexpected change is possible. His speech applies to Merton as well and offers additional insight into his foray into Celtic spirituality: "There is a tide in the affairs of men which when taken at the flood leads on to fortune . . .

43. Merton, "From Pilgrimage to Crusade," 190.

44. Merton, *Search for Solitude*, 381, quoted by Pramuk, *Sophia*, 169.

On such a full sea are we now afloat, and we must take the current when it serves, or lose our ventures."[45]

Immersing himself in Celtic history, culture, literature, and monasticism was, for Merton, the flood that "leads on to fortune." Friendship with Allchin and Chadwick, complemented by books from more than twenty other writers, became Merton's academic tutors who created a "full sea" on which to ride the current. The story of Brendan, in particular, was the inspiration for Merton's own casting off the ropes to launch out into the depths of silence and contemplation. Merton was a new spiritual Brendan, seeking the "divinely appointed place, which was to be the place of ultimate meeting with God." Celtic monasticism offered the appropriate liminal space to affirm Merton's stance as an exile, a bystander. Moreover, it supported the inner *peregrinatio*—that inner voyage on a sea of revelation—to which he was committed.

From Longing to Belonging

Paging through Merton's journals for the 1940s and '50s, the reader can discover several instances when Merton is longing for stability. Orphaned before he was sixteen, Merton was always a seeker, sometimes a drifter, but always a seeker for his identity and his home. Certainly his close friends at Columbia—Bob Lax, Ed Rice, Ad Reinhardt, Bob Gibney, Sy Freedgood— provided a measure of human steadiness. His conversion to Roman Catholicism in 1938 welcomed him into the home of Mother Church, and his entrance into the Trappist monastery in Kentucky enclosed him within the "four walls of my new freedom."[46] But these events were primarily external comforts. The challenge of spiritually growing, of discovering the riches of contemplation, drew Merton ever more into the life of God. Consequently, each time he writes in his journal a variation of "I have finally found what I was looking for,"[47] we can remind ourselves that the spiritual journey is always incomplete. Landing somewhere is only temporary. Perhaps this is why Merton was so captivated by *peregrinatio* and the Brendan story. "Seeking the place of one's resurrection" is a risky journey into the unknown. So many handwritten notes on Brendan's voyage, on *peregrinatio*, and on Abraham as the model for monastic martyrdom suggest that Merton was

45. Shakespeare, *Julius Caesar*, 4.3.218–24.

46. Merton, *Seven Storey Mountain*, 372.

47. See Merton, *Turning Toward the World*, 79–80 and 244 as examples.

indeed finding himself and finding his way to *le point vierge,* that inner "point of nothingness and of absolute poverty [that] is the pure glory of God in us."[48] His original longing was slowly being transformed into a deep sense of belonging, or as John Muir, the American "nature hermit" phrased it: "going out, I found, was really going in."[49]

Merton's physical travels had taken him from Prades, France, to Long Island, to Bermuda, to St-Antonin and Montauban, France, to Ripley Court, Oakham, and Cambridge, England, to Rome, Italy, New York City, Cuba, Olean, and the monastic enclosure of Gethsemani—and beyond that to the surrounding Kentucky knobs, the tool shed he named "St. Anne," and the cinder-block hermitage he dubbed "Our Lady of Carmel," and to his final pilgrimage to Asia. Merton's spiritual *peregrinatio* was much more subtle, yet marked by events that signified major interior changes: learning monastic discipline and contemplation, praying beyond the cloister confines after June 1949, the grace of priesthood, his responsibility for the scholastics, the Fourth and Walnut discovery that he was not fleeing the world but embracing the Christ in all these men and women, his well-researched conferences for the novices, and his commitment to listen to a voice calling him to greater silence and solitude in the wilderness. In that solitude, Merton recognized the Celtic monastic ideal as his own vocation: a little hut in the woods, simple fare, ascetic life, harmony with the environment, clarity of vision, sympathy and love for wild life.[50] Merton's journal entries after he has been given permission to spend more time at the hermitage reveal his joy and peace in this new solitude, and his commitment to developing an "ecological conscience."[51] He enjoys the tiny myrtle warblers "playing and diving for insects" in the pine boughs overhead, "so close I could almost touch them . . . Sense of total kinship with them as if they and I were of the same nature, and as if that nature were nothing but love. And what else but love keeps us all together in being?"[52] A few days later he writes: "This is my full day at the hermitage. No question whatever that this is the kind of schedule to live by . . . Only here do I feel that my life is fully *human.*"[53] And two weeks later: "In solitude everything has its weight for good or evil,

---

48. Merton, *Conjectures,* 142.

49. Muir, *John of the Mountains,* 439.

50. Jackson, *Studies in Early Celtic Nature Poetry,* 96–99.

51. Aldo Leopold's phrase. See Merton, "The Wild Places," in *Selected Essays,* 442–51.

52. Merton, *Dancing in the Water of Life,* 162.

53. Ibid., 169–70.

and one must attend carefully to everything . . . Though now, as a result of solitude, the psalms in choir and especially the hymns and antiphons (Advent!!) have all their old juice and much more too, a new mystery."[54]

In short, the challenge Merton discovers is how to *live* the Celtic *peregrinatio*, how to embrace the overlap of the temporal and the eternal, the external and the internal that is central to the monastic vision and that requires a spiritual journey to discover that "point of nothingness" where God dwells. A. H. Hawkins has pointed out that this spiritual challenge can be thought of as *epektasis*, so central to fourth-century Gregory of Nyssa's teaching which Merton appropriated. *Epektasis* is a drawing of the soul ever onward or upward toward God so that one becomes more and more like God.[55] St. Paul captures the dynamism of this quest with his concise admission: "I press on toward the goal."[56] Such a *peregrinatio,* maintains Hawkins, is not linear, or cyclical, but like Yeats' widening gyre,[57] it is spiral.

We see an illustration of this spiral journey in Merton's early years when he was immersed in worldly pleasures at Columbia, chooses the austerity of a Trappist monastery to leave the world behind, and then experiences his epiphany on Fourth and Walnut Streets in which he sees in a new way his connection with people and the importance of having compassion *for* the world. Hawkins points out that Merton's favorite childhood books were *Greek Heroes* and a geography book linked with "travel, adventure, the wide sea, and unlimited possibilities of human heroism, with myself as the hero."[58] This seems so like the voyages of Bran, Maeldun, and Brendan. Yet Merton's spiritual *peregrinatio* was not seeking a destination, nor was he the hero of the action; rather, Merton's interior *peregrinatio* was a "dialectical movement from one idea to its opposite at a higher unity"—a spiral.[59] The words with which Merton closes his autobiography are not merely a literary finale but a prophetic insight to be lived into: "*Sit finis libri, non finis quaerendi*" [Let this be the end of the book, not of the searching"].[60] In poetic terms, the challenge of Merton's unique spiral *peregrinatio*—or living out of

---

54. Ibid., 176.

55. Hawkins, *Archetypes of Conversion,* 117–18.

56. Phil 3:14, NRSV.

57. Yeats, "The Second Coming."

58. Merton, *Seven Storey Mountain,* 11, quoted by Hawkins, *Archetypes of Conversion,* 127.

59. Hawkins, *Archetypes of Conversion,* 119, quoted by Pearson, "Celtic Monasticism."

60. Merton, *Seven Storey Mountain,* 423.

a "transfigured centre"—is to discover how to actualize T. S. Eliot's words in *Four Quartets*: "We shall not cease from exploration, and the end of all our exploring will be to arrive where we started and know the place for the first time."[61]

To "know the place for the first time" requires a new way of seeing; to discover how to live out of a "transfigured centre" where the temporal and the eternal, the external and the internal are blended is to see one's life precisely focused within a new reality. Through his study of Celtic history and monasticism, his fondness for the *Navigatio Sancti Brendani*, and his delight in the personal relationship of the Irish hermits to their natural surroundings, Merton saw reality and his monastic vocation in a new light. No wonder he could say he had "decided to marry the silence of the forest."[62] His growing sensitivity to the environment and awareness of our responsibility to protect it reinforced Merton's determination to embrace all of creation. The confluence of his extensive knowledge of Eastern traditions, his personal interaction with Celtic scholars, and his rich delving into the experience of wholeness that intimacy with the Celts provided affirmed not only Merton's desire for deeper solitude and silence but also his attraction to the hermit life.

The specific characteristics of Celtic Christianity, enumerated by Paul Pearson in a lecture for Iona College, were especially attractive to Merton: an attitude toward nature that reveals the manifold characteristics of God; hospitality and openness to other faiths and cultures; resemblance to the self-discipline of both the Desert Fathers and the Zen masters; a rich literary and artistic culture that reverences beauty, and the unique asceticism of inner and outer pilgrimage or *peregrinatio*.[63] While these are indeed central characteristics of Celtic Christianity, I want to extend these characteristics to suggest reasons for Merton's affinity for Celtic Christianity and, in particular, Celtic monasticism. These reasons, though not inherent in Celtic Christianity itself, nevertheless fulfill Merton's deepest desires and enable him to experience the "full seas" of life.

First, the imaginative worldview of the Celts, especially the imaginative power of the Irish monks, demonstrated for Merton the possibility of living a vocation caught up in the Trinitarian unity of God, humanity, and earth. The all-pervasive attention to the Holy Trinity that blessed not only

61. Eliot, "Little Gidding," in *Four Quartets*, 39.

62. Merton, *Day of a Stranger*, 49.

63. Pearson, "Sentinels."

sacred actions, but also common rituals of the home signaled for Merton a unified worldview and existence that could lead to new levels of wholeness. Second, the Celtic tradition of monks and recluses with a "rootedness in a vision of a world made whole and infused with the Divine"[64] affirmed Merton's call to lead the life of a hermit associated with the monastery at Gethsemani—a decision that Professor Nora Chadwick applauded: "It is lovely to think that in this modern world there are still spirits attuned to the contemplative life."[65] A decision that prompted Merton to respond: "on the whole I see that it is the best life there is. At least for me. . . one feels close to the root of things."[66] Two combined and unpublished holographic notebooks attest to Merton's extensive interest in and research into the lives of Celtic recluses, Irish anchorages, the writings of the Italian Benedictine St. Peter Damian, and Rules for Recluses and English Eremitism.[67] Merton's various essays on eremitism, written during this time and eventually printed in *Contemplation in a World of Action,* substantiate his serious investigation of the solitary life and desire to pursue it for himself. Indeed, a whole new world was "opening up." Third, Celtic Christianity offered not an aberrant perspective, but a model of theological integrity, grounded in a lively Latin culture, notable artistic achievement, and the wisdom of the East. Merton saw the possibility of that paradoxical union of East and West he so ardently desired already manifested in Celtic monasticism. Fourth, the unique Celtic "take" on *peregrinatio* opened a new horizon for Merton who already saw himself as a pilgrim, a bystander, a stranger, an exile. Becoming an exile or pilgrim for the sake of God was a tempting invitation for Merton who from his youth had been a physical wanderer. The tradition of *peregrinatio* and Merton's enthusiasm for the *Navigatio Sancti Brendani* gave him an added rationale for "casting off the ropes" and setting himself adrift on the ocean of God's mercy—hopefully inaugurating a new "golden age" of eremitic monasticism. Fifth, Merton's fascination with Celtic hermit poetry revealed an "affinity between his own life as a solitary in the Gethsemani woods and the lives of these Celtic monks."[68] One has only to read his journals of 1964–68 to realize how important nature, especially the deer

---

64. Ibid., 14.

65. Chadwick, unpublished letter to Merton, May 28, 1966, Louisville, KY: Thomas Merton Center.

66. Merton, *School of Charity,* 308.

67. Merton, *Working Notebooks* #53 and 54.

68. Pearson, "Sentinels," 9.

near the hermitage, had become to Merton. As Merton wrote in his account of a day in his hermitage when he was given permission to live in the little cinderblock house permanently:

> I live in the woods as a reminder that I am free not to be a number . . . Do I spend my day in a "place"? I know there are trees here. I know there are birds here. I know the birds in fact very well, for there are precise pairs of birds (two of each of fifteen or twenty species) living in the immediate area of my cabin. I share this particular place with them: we form an ecological balance. This harmony gives the idea of "place" a new configuration.[69]

Whereas Merton regarded monastic life as a "hot medium," he believed "the hermit life is cool. It is a life of low definition in which there is little to decide, in which there are few transactions or none, in which there are no packages to be delivered . . . It is not intense. There is no give and take of questions and answers, problems and solutions."[70]

In a profound way and at a very deep level, Merton discovered himself in Celtic Christianity and, especially, in Celtic monasticism. He saw a mirror of his life and desires in these ancient monks living on "water and herbs," expressing kinship with all of creation, and writing poems about the birds overhead. Early Celtic monasticism, with its roots in third-century Egypt and the East, spoke eloquently to this twentieth-century monk who longed for more solitude. Their asceticism resonated with his own spiritual discipline and hermitage rituals: "Washing out the coffee pot in the rain bucket" and "Approaching the outhouse with circumspection" to avoid the resident king snake.[71] The celebration of the liturgy of birds echoed his own experience of the "full meaning of Lauds" under the trees in the woods. And the Celts' openness and hospitality to the stranger reaffirmed his own sense of the human community and prompted his challenge to our generation in the final paragraphs of his essay "From Pilgrimage to Crusade," which he regarded as "central to his thought." Merton could not have been more clear about the mission facing us, a mission traceable perhaps to the beginnings of Christianity in Ireland and the lands ruled by the Celts, and somehow not yet accomplished in our world:

69. Merton, *Day of a Stranger*, 33.

70. Ibid., 37.

71. Ibid., 53.

Our task now is to learn that if we can voyage to the ends of the earth and there find *ourselves* in the aborigine who most differs from ourselves, we will have made a fruitful pilgrimage . . . We have to come to the end of a long journey and see that the stranger we meet there is no other than ourselves—which is the same as saying that we find Christ in him.[72]

72. Merton, "From Pilgrimage to Crusade," 204.

Bibliography

Adam, David. *A Desert in the Ocean: The Spiritual Journey According to St. Brendan the Navigator*. New York: Paulist, 2000.

———. *The Open Gate: Celtic Prayers for Growing Spirituality*. Harrisburg, PA: Morehouse, 1995.

Allchin, A. M. *Ann Griffiths*. Writers of Wales. Cardiff: University of Wales Press, 1976.

———. "Can We Do Wales Then?" *The Merton Journal* 13/2 (Advent 2006) 2–10.

———. *God's Presence Makes the World: The Celtic Vision through the Centuries in Wales*. London: Darton, Longman & Todd, 1997.

———. "Our Lives, a Powerful Pentecost: Merton's Meeting with Russian Christianity." *The Merton Annual* 11 (1998) 33–48.

———. *Songs To Her God: Spirituality of Ann Griffiths*. Cambridge, MA: Cowley, 1987.

———. "The Worship of the Whole Creation: Merton and the Eastern Fathers." *The Merton Annual* 5 (1992) 189–204.

Auden, W. H. *The Enchafèd Flood or The Romantic Iconography of the Sea*. London: Faber & Faber, 1951.

Beasts and Saints. Translated by Helen Waddell. London: Constable, 1934.

Benedict. *The Rule of St. Benedict*. Translated by D. Oswald Hunter Blair. 4th ed. Fort Augustus, Scotland: Abbey, 1934.

Bernard of Clairvaux. *The Letters of St. Bernard of Clairvaux*. Translated by Bruno Scott James. Chicago: Regnery, 1953.

Best, Richard Irvine, and Hugh Jackson Lawlor, eds. *The Martyrology of Tallaght: From the Book of Leinster & MS 5100-4 in the Royal Library, Brussels*. Brussels: Harrison, 1931.

Beuchner Frederick. *Brendan*. New York: Atheneum, 1987.

Bidgood, Ruth. "Hymn to San Ffraid." In *Symbols of Plenty*, 1–20. Norwich, UK: Canterbury 2006.

Blake, William. *The Poetry and Prose of William Blake*. Edited by David V. Erdman, Garden City, NY: Doubleday, 1970.

Bolshakoff, Sergius. *Russian Mystics*. Introduction by Thomas Merton. Kalamazoo: Cistercian, 1977.

Bourgeault, Cynthia. "The Monastic Archetype in the *Navigatio* of St. Brendan." *Monastic Studies* 14 (1983) 109.

———. *The Wisdom of Jesus: Transforming Heart and Mind—A New Perspective on Christ and His Message*. Boston: Shambala, 2008.

Bradley, Ian. *Celtic Christianity: Making Myths and Chasing Dreams*. New York: St. Martin's, 1988.

Bray, Dorothy Ann. "A Note on the Life of St. Brendan." *Cistercian Studies* 20 (1985) 14–20.

Buechner, Frederick. *Brendan*. New York: Atheneum, 1978.

Carmichael, Alexander, ed. *Carmina Gadelica, Hymns and Incantations, with Illustrative Notes of Words, Rites and Customs Dying and Obsolete*. Schottish Academic Press, 1900.

Chadwick, Nora K. *The Age of Saints in the Early Celtic Church*. London: Oxford University Press, 1961.

———. "Mission to Ireland." In *The Fires of Faith*, edited by Friedrich Heer, 23–27. Verona: Arnoldo Mondadori Editore, 1970.

———. *Poetry and Letters in Early Christian Gaul*. London: Bowes and Bowes, 1955.

———. *Poetry and Prophecy*. Cambridge: Cambridge University Press, 1942.

Collins, John. "The BC Connection: Thomas Merton and the Boston College Jesuits." *The Merton Seasonal* 36/1 (Spring 2011) 19–33.

Colson, Chuck. "Learning from the Irish." March 17, 2008. http://www.breakpoint.org/bpcommentaries/entry/13/10514.

Consedine, Raphael. "Trasna." *Songs of the Journey*, 45. St. Kilda West, Aust.: Presentation Sisters Victoria, 2001.

Cousineau, Phil. *The Art of Pilgrimage: The Seeker's Guide to Making Travel Sacred*. Berkeley, CA: Conari, 1998.

Daggy, Robert E. "Thomas Merton and the Search for Owen Merton." In *The Vision of Thomas Merton*, edited by Patrick F. O'Connell, 23–41. Notre Dame: Ave Maria, 2003.

Dart, Ron. "Thomas Merton: Hedgehog and Fox." *The Merton Seasonal* 40/1 (Spring 2015) 14–16.

Dauwer, Ellen. "What New Concepts are Yet to Emerge?" *Praying in These Emerging Times*, edited by Annemarie Sanders, 6. Silver Spring, MD: LCWR, 2014.

Davies, Oliver. "Thomas Merton and Meister Eckhart." *The Merton Journal* 4/2 (Advent 1997) 15–24.

Davies, Oliver, and Thomas O'Loughlin, eds. *Celtic Spirituality*. New York: Paulist, 1999.

De Waal, Esther. *The Celtic Alternative: A Reminder of the Christianity We Lost*. London: Rider, 1987.

———. *The Celtic Way of Prayer: The Recovery of the Religious Imagination*. Garden City, NY: Doubleday, 1997.

———. *Every Earthly Blessing: Rediscovering the Celtic Tradition*. Harrisburg, PA: Morehouse, 1991.

———. "A Fresh Look at the Synod of Whitby: A Mark of Unity and Reconciliation." In *I Have Called You Friends: Reflections on Reconciliation: in Honor of Frank T. Griswold*, edited by Barbara Braver, 29–43. Cambridge, MA: Cowley, 2006.

———. "An Introduction to Celtic Spirituality." February 2, 2014. http://www.stpauls.co.uk/View-St. Pauls-Videos.

———. *A World Made Whole: Rediscovering the Celtic Tradition*. London: Fount, 1991.

Dunn, Joseph. "The Brendan Problem." *The Catholic Historical Review* 6/4 (January 1921) 395–477.

Egeria. *Egeria: Diary of a Pilgrimage*. Translated by George E. Gringras. New York: Newman, 1970.

Eliot, T. S. *Four Quartets*. New York: Harcourt, Brace & World, 1943.

Flower, Robin. *The Irish Tradition.* Oxford: Clarendon, 1947.

Francis I. "First General Audience." March 28, 2013. http://www.catholicworldreport. com/Blog/2131/full_text_pope_francis_first_general_auience_address.aspx.

Gerald of Wales. *The Journey through Wales and The Description of Wales.* Translated by Lewis Thorpe. London: Penguin, 1978.

Gougaud, Louis. *Christianity in Celtic Lands.* Translated by Maude Joynt. London, 1932.

Griffith, Ann. *Hymns.* Translated by H. A. Hodges. Cardiff. http://www.anngriffiths. cardiff.ac.uk/.

Guigo I. *The Solitary Life: A Letter of Guigo to a Friend.* Translated by Thomas Merton. Worcester, UK: Stanbrook Abbey, 1963.

Hart, Patrick. "Eremitism in the Celtic Church." *Cistercian Studies* 3 (1968) 124–36.

Hawkins, Anne Hunsaker. *Archetypes of Conversion.* Lewisburg, PA: Bucknell University Press, 1985.

Hempstead-Milton, Sheila. "Emblems of Birds: Birds as a Symbol of Grace in Three Poems of Thomas Merton." *The Merton Seasonal* 18/1 (Winter 1993) 16–24.

Hodges, H. A. *Homage to Ann Griffiths.* Penarth: Church in Wales, 1976.

Hopkins, Gerard Manley. *The Poems of Gerard Manley Hopkins.* Edited by W. H. Gardner and N. H. MacKenzie. 4th ed. New York: Oxford University Press, 1948.

Horan, Daniel P. *The Franciscan Heart of Thomas Merton.* Notre Dame: Ave Maria, 2014.

Hughes, Kathleen. "The Changing Theory and Practice of Irish Pilgrimage." *The Journal of Ecclesiastical History* 11/2 (October 1960) 143–51.

Jackson, Kenneth, H. *A Celtic Miscellany.* Cambridge, MA: Harvard University Press, 1951.

———. *Studies in Early Celtic Nature Poetry.* Cambridge: Cambridge University Press, 1935.

Kenny, James F. *Sources for the Early History of Ireland.* Vol. 1. New York: Columbia University Press, 1929.

Kilcourse, George. "A Shy Wild Deer: The 'True Self' in Thomas Merton's Poetry." *The Merton Annual* 4 (1991) 97–109.

Kingsley, Charles. *The Hermits.* Whitefish, MT: Kessinger, 2010.

Knight, Sarah Kemble. "The Journal of Madam Knight." In *The Heath Anthology of American Literature,* edited by Paul Lauter et al., 608–26. 6th ed. Boston: Wadsworth, 2009.

Knowles, David. *Christian Monasticism.* New York: McGraw-Hill, 1969.

Lakoff, George, and Mark Johnson. *Metaphors We Live By.* Chicago: University of Chicago Press, 1980.

Lentfoehr, Thérèse. *Words and Silence: On the Poetry of Thomas Merton.* New York: New Directions, 1979.

Mackey, James P. *Introduction to Celtic Christianity.* Edinburgh: T. & T. Clark, 1989.

Macquarrie, John. *Paths in Spirituality.* New York: Harper & Row, 1972.

Marier, Theodore, ed. *St. Pius X Hymnal.* Boston: McLaughlin and Reilly, 1953.

Merton, Ruth Jenkins. *Tom's Book: To Granny with Tom's Best Love.* Edited by Sheila Milton. Monteray, KY: Larkspur, 2005.

Merton, Thomas. "Anthology of Irish Poetry." Unpublished mimeograph in *Collected Essays* 2 (September 1964) 232–54. Louisville: Thomas Merton Center.

———. "Art and Worship." *Sponsa Regis* (December 1959) 114–17.

———. *Ascent to Truth.* New York: Harcourt, Brace, 1951.

————. *The Asian Journal of Thomas Merton.* Edited by Naomi Burton, Patrick Hart, and Jay Loughlin. New York: New Directions: 1973.

————. *The Behavior of Titans.* New York: New Directions, 1961.

————. *Cassian and the Fathers: Initiation into the Monastic Tradition.* Edited by Patrick F. O'Connell. Kalamazoo, MI: Cistercian, 2005.

————. "The Cell." In *Contemplation in a World of Action,* 252–59. Garden City, NY: Doubleday, 1973.

————. "Christian Solitude." In *Contemplation in a World of Action,* 237–51. Garden City, NY: Doubleday, 1973.

————. *The Collected Poems of Thomas Merton.* New York: New Directions, 1977.

————. *Conjectures of a Guilty Bystander.* New York: Doubleday, 1966.

————. *Contemplation in a World of Action.* Garden City, NY: Doubleday, 1971.

————. *The Courage for Truth: Letters to Writers.* Edited by Christine M. Bochen. New York: Farrar, Straus & Giroux, 1993.

————. *Dancing in the Water of Life: Seeking Peace in the Hermitage.* Edited by Robert E. Daggy. San Francisco: Harper Collins, 1997.

————. *Entering the Silence: Becoming a Monk and Writer.* Edited by Jonathan Montaldo. San Francisco: Harper Collins, 1996.

————. "From Pilgrimage to Crusade." In *Thomas Merton: Selected Essays,* edited by Patrick F. Connell, 185–204. Maryknoll, NY: Orbis, 2013.

————. *The Geography of Lograire.* New York: New Directions, 1968.

————. *The Hidden Ground of Love: The Letters of Thomas Merton on Religious Experience and Social Concerns.* Edited by William H. Shannon. New York: Farrar, Straus & Giroux, 1985.

————. *An Introduction to Christian Mysticism: Initiation into the Monastic Tradition 3.* Edited by Patrick F. O'Connell. Kalamazoo, MI: Cistercian, 2008.

————. *Learning to Love: Exploring Solitude and Freedom.* Edited by Christine M. Bochen. San Francisco: Harper Collins, 1997.

————. *Literary Essays of Thomas Merton.* Edited by Patrick Hart. New York: New Directions, 1981.

————. *Mystics and Zen Masters.* New York: Farrar, Straus & Giroux, 1967.

————. *New Seeds of Contemplation.* New York: New Directions, 1962.

————. "Notes and Sentences." E.1.Unpublished holographic notes (possibly from May 1951). Louisville KY: Thomas Merton Center.

————. *The Other Side of the Mountain: The End of the Journey.* Edited by Patrick Hart. San Francisco: Harper Collins, 1998.

————. *Pre-Benedictine Monasticism: Initiation into the Monastic Tradition 2.* Edited by Patrick F. O'Connell. Kalamazoo, MI: Cistercian, 2006.

————. *Raids on the Unspeakable.* New York: New Directions, 1964.

————. *Recorded Conferences.* Louisville: Thomas Merton Center.

41.2 "Monastic spirituality: life as a journey." 1/16/63.

41.4 "Monastic spirituality: the way." 1/30/63.

99.4 "Aetheria's pilgrimage." 2/2/64.

102.3 "Origins of Celtic monasticism." 5/17/64.

106.2 "Distractions in prayer and the desert fathers' remedy; Irish monasticism." 6/14/64.

124.2 "Early Celtic art. Machine age and monastic culture." 9/5/64.

125.1 "Early Irish monastic art." 9/12/64.

125.4 "Irish art." 9/19/64.

175.2 "Irish monks. Points on the mystic life in the Far East, Nirvana." 3/10/68.

175.3 "Irish monks on mystic life." 3/25/68.

———. Review of *Les Chrétientés Celtiques*, by Olivier Loyer. *Collectanea Cisterciensia* 29 (1967) # 140, 78–79; *Cistercian Studies* 3.4 (1968) #189, 119–20.

———. *The Road to Joy: Letters to New and Old Friends*. Edited by Robert E. Daggy. New York: Farrar, Straus, & Giroux, 1989.

———. *The School of Charity: Letters of Thomas Merton on Religious Renewal and Spiritual Direction*. Edited by Patrick Hart. New York: Farrar, Straus, & Giroux, 1990.

———. *A Search for Solitude: Pursuing the Monk's True Life*. Edited by Lawrence S. Cunningham. San Francisco: Harper Collins, 1996.

———. *The Seven Storey Mountain*. New York: Harcourt, Brace, 1948.

———. *Thomas Merton: Selected Essays*. Edited by Patrick F. O'Connell. Maryknoll, NY: Orbis, 2013.

———. *Thoughts in Solitude*. New York: Farrar, Straus & Cudahy, 1958.

———. *Turning Toward the World: The Pivotal Years*. Edited by Victor A. Kramer. San Francisco: Harper Collins, 1996.

———. *The Waters of Siloe*. New York: Harcourt, Brace, 1949.

———. *The Wisdom of the Desert*. New York: New Directions, 1960.

———. *Witness to Freedom: Letters of Times of Crisis*. Edited by William H. Shannon. New York: Farrar, Straus & Giroux, 1994.

———. *Working Notebook #14* (June 1964). Unpublished holograph. Louisville: Thomas Merton Center.

———. *Working Notebook #15* (1965–August 1966). Unpublished holograph. Louisville: Thomas Merton Center.

———. *Working Notebook #18* (1966–67). Unpublished holograph. Louisville: Thomas Merton Center.

———. *Working Notebook #24* (November 1966–June 67) Unpublished holograph. Louisville: Thomas Merton Center.

———. *Working Notebook #48* (no date; 1966?) Unpublished holograph. Louisville: Thomas Merton Center.

———. *Working Notebooks #53, 54* (1966–1967) Unpublished holograph. Louisville: Thomas Merton Center.

———. *Zen and the Birds of Appetite*. New York: New Directions, 1968.

Meyer, Kuno. *Ancient Irish Poetry*. London: Constable, 1913.

———. *Selections from Ancient Irish Poetry*. London: Constable, 1911.

Moore, T. M. *Celtic Flame: The Burden of Patrick*. N.p.: Xlibris, 2000.

———. "Glory All Around." February 18, 2008. http://www.breakpoint.org/features-columns/archive/1240-glory-all-around.

Morewood, Michael. *Praying a New Story*. Maryknoll, NY: Orbis, 2004.

Mott, Michael. *The Seven Mountains of Thomas Merton*. Boston: Houghton Mifflin, 1984.

Muir, John. *John of the Mountains: The Unpublished Journals*. Edited by Linnie Marsh Wolfe. Madison: University of Wisconsin Press, 1938.

Newell, J. Philip. *Christ of the Celts: The Healing of Creation*. San Francisco: Jossey-Bass, 2008.

———. *Listening for the Heartbeat of God: A Celtic Spirituality*. New York: Paulist, 1997.

———. *One Foot in Eden: A Celtic View of the Stages of Life*. New York: Paulist, 1999.

O'Connell, Patrick F., ed. *The Vision of Thomas Merton*. Notre Dame: Ave Maria, 2003.

O'Donohue, John. *A Celtic Pilgrimage with John O'Donohue*. DVD. New York: SoundsTrue, 2009.

O'Loughlin, Thomas. *Journeys on the Edge: The Celtic Tradition*. Maryknoll, NY: Orbis, 2000.

O'Malley, Brendan, ed. *A Celtic Primer: The Complete Celtic Resource and Collection*. Harrisburg, PA: Morehouse, 2002.

O'Riordain, John J. *The Music of What Happens: Celtic Spirituality*. Dublin: Columba, 1996.

Panikkar, Raimon. *Blessed Simplicity: The Monk as Universal Archetype*. New York: Seebury, 1982.

Pearson, Paul M. "Celtic Monasticism as a Metaphor for Thomas Merton's Journey." *Merton Center Occasional Papers* 2. October 24, 2003. http://merton.org/papers/celtic.htm.

———. "Merton and the Celtic Monastic Tradition: Search for the Promised Land." *The Merton Annual* 5 (1992) 263–77.

———. "'Sentinels Upon the World's Frontier': Thomas Merton and Celtic Monasticism." Lecture for Iona College, New Rochelle, NY, April 2013.

Pelaguis. "Letter to Demetrias." In *Letters of Pelagius and His Followers*, edited and translated by B. R. Reed, 29–70. Suffolk, UK: Boydell, 1991.

Perrin, David B. *Studying Christian Spirituality*. London: Routledge, 2007.

Plummer, Charles. *Irish Litanies*. London: Harrison, 1925.

Powers, Jessica. "Abraham." In *Selected Poetry of Jessica Powers*, edited by Regina Siegfried and Robert Morneau, 6. Washington, DC: ICS, 1999.

Pramuk, Christopher. *Sophia: The Hidden Christ of Thomas Merton*. Collegeville, MN: Liturgical, 2009.

The Qur'an. Translated by Abdullah Yusuf Ali. Elmhurst, NY: Tahrike Tarsile Qur'an, 2008.

Richardson, Kerry. *Celtic Calligraphy: Calligraphy, Knotwork and Illumination*. Tunbridge Wells, UK: Search, 2014.

Ryan, John. *Irish Monasticism*. Ithaca, NY: Cornell University Press, 1931.

Sanders, Scott Russell. "Telling the Holy." In *Staying Put: Making a Home in a Restless World*, 143–69. Boston: Beacon, 1993.

Sellner, Edward. *Wisdom of the Celtic Saints*. Notre Dame: Ave Maria, 1993.

Severin, Tim. *The Brendan Voyage*. New York: McGraw-Hill, 1978.

Scutchfield, F. Douglas, and Paul Evans Holbrook Jr., eds. *The Letters of Thomas Merton and Victor and Carolyn Hammer*. Lexington: University Press of Kentucky, 2014.

Shakespeare, William. *The Riverside Shakespeare*. Edited by G. Blakemore Evans et al. Boston: Houghton Mifflin, 1974.

Shannon, William H. *Silent Lamp: The Thomas Merton Story*. New York: Crossroad, 1992.

Shannon, William H., Christine M. Bochen, and Patrick F. O'Connell, eds. *The Thomas Merton Encyclopedia*. Maryknoll, NY: Orbis, 2002.

Stewart, Columba. *Cassian the Monk*. New York: Oxford University Press, 1998.

Stommes, Mary, ed. *Give Us this Day: Daily Prayer for Today's Catholic*. Collegeville, MN: Liturgical, n.d.

Sullivan, Robert. "In St. Brendan's Wake." *Attaché: U. S Airways* (March 2001) 66–72.

Szabo, Lynn. *In the Dark Before Dawn: New Selected Poems of Thomas Merton*. New York: New Directions, 2005.

Thomas, R. S. "A Welsh Testament." In *Collected Poems, 1945–1990*, 117–18. London: Orion, 1993.

Thurston, Bonnie Bowman. *Belonging to Borders: A Sojourn in the Celtic Tradition.* Collegeville, MN: Liturgical, 2011.

Ward, Benedicta. *A True Easter: The Synod of Whitby 664 AD.* Oxford: SLG, 2007.

Warner, Keith Douglas. "Get Him Out of the Birdbath! What Does It Mean to Have a Patron Saint of Ecology?" In *Franciscan Theology of the Environment*, edited by Dawn M. Nothwehr, 361–75. Quincy, IL: Franciscan, 2003.

Weiner, Eric. "Where Heaven and Earth Come Closer." *New York Times*, TR10, March 11, 2010.

Weis, Monica. *The Environmental Vision of Thomas Merton.* Lexington: University Press of Kentucky, 2011.

Whitsel, Montague. "The Voyage Theme in Celtic Mythology." montaguewhitsel.blogspot. com/p/voyage-theme-in-celtic-mythology.html.

Woodcock, George. *Thomas Merton: Monk and Poet.* Vancouver, BC: Douglas & McIntyre, 1978.

Wordsworth, William. "Lines Composed a Few Miles above Tintern Abbey." In *William Wordsworth: Selected Poems and Prefaces*, edited by Jack Stillinger, 108–11. Boston: Houghton Mifflin, 1965.

Yeats, W. B. "The Second Coming." In *The Collected Poems of W. B. Yeats, 1889–1939*, 186–87. N.p. https://archive.org/stream/WBYeats-CollectedPoems1889-1939#page/n199/mode/2up.

Index